D0327365

The Future of the Financial Exchanges

The Elsevier and Mondo Visione World Capital Markets Series

ELSEVIER

mondovisione
Worldwide Exchange Intelligence

Series Editor: Herbie Skeete

The Elsevier and Mondo Visione World Capital Markets Series consists of books that cover the developments in the capital markets, as well as basic texts introducing the markets to those working directly or indirectly in the capital markets. Investors are more knowledgeable and demanding than ever before and there is a thirst for information by professional investors and those who sell and provide services to them. Regulators are demanding more transparency, and new rules and regulations are being introduced constantly. The impact of competition means that markets are constantly changing and merging, and new instruments are being devised. The Series provides cutting-edge information and discussion about these and other developments affecting the capital markets. Technology underpins and is driving innovation in the markets. Inappropriate technology or no technology can bring down even the soundest financial institution. This series therefore also includes books that enable market experts to understand aspects of technology that are driving the markets.

Books in the Series include:

- *The Future of the Financial Exchanges* by Herbie Skeete
- *Managing Financial Information in the Trade Lifecycle* by Martijn Groot
- *MDDL and the Quest for a Market Data Standard* by Martin Sexton
- *Market Data Explained* by Marc Alvarez

Series Editor Herbie Skeete is a well-known figure in the financial information industry, having spent twenty-six years at Reuters. During his many senior positions with Reuters—most recently as Head of Equities Content and Head of Exchange Strategy—Mr. Skeete has become recognized globally as an expert on exchanges and content issues. He is frequently asked to address conferences and to contribute to roundtable discussions. Mr. Skeete runs the exchange information publisher Mondo Visione Ltd, edits the industry-standard *Handbook of World Stock, Derivative & Commodity Exchanges*, and operates the exchange information website www.exchange-handbook.com

The Future of the Financial Exchanges

Insights and Analysis from The Mondo Visione Exchange Forum

Herbie Skeete

ELSEVIER

AMSTERDAM • BOSTON • HEIDELBERG
LONDON • NEW YORK • OXFORD • PARIS
SAN DIEGO • SAN FRANCISCO
SINGAPORE • SYDNEY • TOKYO

mondovisione
Worldwide Exchange Intelligence

HG
3821
.S54
2009

30 Corporate Drive, Suite 400, Burlington, MA 01803, USA
525 B Street, Suite 1900, San Diego, California 92101-4495, USA
84 Theobald's Road, London WC1X 8RR, UK

Copyright © 2009 Mondo Visione, Ltd. Published by Elsevier Ltd. All rights reserved.

No part of this publication may be reproduced or transmitted in any form or by any means, electronic or mechanical, including photocopy, recording, or any information storage and retrieval system, without permission in writing from the publisher.

Permissions may be sought directly from Elsevier's Science & Technology Rights Department in Oxford, UK: phone: (+44) 1865 843830, fax: (+44) 1865 853333, E–mail: permissions@elsevier.com. You may also complete your request online via the Elsevier homepage (http://elsevier.com), by selecting "Support & Contact" then "Copyright and Permission" and then "Obtaining Permissions."

Library of Congress Cataloging-in-Publication Data
Application Submitted

British Library Cataloguing-in-Publication Data
A catalogue record for this book is available from the British Library.

ISBN: 978-0-12-374421-0

For information on all Elsevier publications
visit our Web site at www.elsevierdirect.com

Printed in the United States of America
08   09   10   9   8   7   6   5   4   3   2   1

Working together to grow
libraries in developing countries

www.elsevier.com | www.bookaid.org | www.sabre.org

ELSEVIER   BOOK AID
              International   Sabre Foundation

Contents

University Libraries
Carnegie Mellon University
Pittsburgh, PA 15213-3890

Preface

Last year, we said the Mondo Visione Exchange Forum was different from other conferences. Some must have wondered if this was just marketing hype. But the response from our participants and publications such as *The Economist* showed us that we had succeeded in putting on an event that people in the exchange industry wanted and needed.

We were determined that delegates would not be subjected to a poorly managed event where the organizers do not understand financial markets and services. We deliberately avoided the tired formula of stilted, recycled, one-way presentations. Instead, panel discussions were deliberately organized to be highly interactive, where contributions from delegates were actively sought and welcomed. Panel sessions were designed to encourage debate and aimed at shaping the future of the sector. Features that made the 2007 conference successful were the outstanding calibre of speakers, drawn from the very highest levels of leading organizations in the exchange and Bourse industry around the world, and the participatory nature of our program, in which interactive, PowerPoint-free panel sessions encouraged the cut and thrust of genuine debate involving panelists and the audience of senior executives.

With the expert chairmanship of my old friend Dr. Benn Steil, Senior Fellow and Director of International Economics at the Council on Foreign Relations, the Mondo Visione Exchange Forum 2007 proved highly successful. He ensured that all contributions were relevant. No one was allowed to use the Mondo Visione Exchange Forum for a blatant sales pitch. Without Benn's contribution, the event would have been infinitely poorer. He ensured that the standards were kept high. We owe Benn and the individual panel Chairs an enormous debt of gratitude.

We have just (June 2008) held a successful 2008 Mondo Visione Exchange Forum at which we examined issues such as the valuation of exchanges as businesses and topical issues, the impact of new entrants challenging traditional exchanges, the rise in commodity prices, and many other burning and topical issues.

We hope that this summary of the 2007 Mondo Visione Exchange Forum gives you a flavor of the event, and we hope one day to be able to welcome you to an Exchange Forum. We promise that you will not be disappointed.

Acknowledgments

We would like to thank Scott Cooper for his skill in editing this book. It is not easy for someone who is not a market practitioner to come to grips with terms such as "dark pools of liquidity," "Smart Order Routing," or "Straight Through Processing." Scott proved more than equal to this task, and we are thankful to him for seeing this project through to the end with his unfailing good humor intact.

With the expert chairmanship of my old friend Dr. Benn Steil, Senior Fellow and Director of International Economics at the Council on Foreign Relations, the Mondo Visione Exchange Forum 2007 proved highly successful. Benn ensured the relevance of all contributions, that they were informative rather than pitches, and maintained standards without which the event would have been infinitely poorer. We owe Benn and the individual panel Chairs an enormous debt of gratitude.

Panel Chairs

Stock Exchanges	Dr. Benn Steil, Senior Fellow and Director of International Economics at the Council on Foreign Relations, New York
Sell-Side and Exchanges	Dr. Benn Steil, Senior Fellow and Director of International Economics at the Council on Foreign Relations, New York
Crossfire	Patrick Young
Buy-Side and Exchanges	Holly Stark, President Efficient Frontiers
Clearing and Settlement	David Hardy, Former CEO LCH. Clearnet

Derivatives Exchanges	Dr. Benn Steil, Senior Fellow and Director of International Economics at the Council on Foreign Relations, New York
Regulators and Exchanges	Paul Arlman, Founding Board Member, European Corporate Governance Institute
Corporate Governance and Socially Responsible Investing	Mark Makepeace, CEO, FTSE Group
Technology and Exchanges	Peter Bennett, Solutions Principal, HCLb Technologies

Chapter 1

Two Decades of Change

Introduction

In May 2007, an extraordinary meeting took place in London: The Exchange Forum. Chief executives from many of the world's most important financial exchanges came together with other leaders from a wide array of global banking, trading, and investing firms, index providers, regulators, system suppliers, and noted academics to discuss the rapidly changing business and technological environment in which exchanges function. The forum was an exclusive event, open only to the most senior-level individuals in the global exchanges community: those who run exchanges, who are clients of exchanges, who invest in exchanges, and who supply goods and services to exchanges.

In presentations and panel discussions over two days, these experts explored the problem of shrinking margins as exchanges add less value to the trading cycle. Participants shared what exchanges are doing today to respond to the challenges wrought by competition, globalization, and rapid technology advances. They also looked to the future and discussed the multiasset, multicurrency, and multiregion trading that holds the promise of future success.

This is a report on this exclusive event that brought together leading exchange professionals, their customers, and suppliers from around the globe to share insights and experiences. We provide an overview of the latest technological, regulatory, and market developments in the exchange industry and the common problems exchanges face; explore some of the ways in which these problems are being addressed; and present the consensus view—from leading exchange professionals—on how to move forward. The ideas here come directly from the world's leading exchange professionals and customers.

To open the discussions, this diverse group began with a quick review of the way the trading process works today and how it has changed. That is where we, too, begin.

BACKGROUND

A lot has changed since the late 13th century, when commodity traders in Bruges would meet informally at the home of a Mr. Van der Beurse. When in 1309 this group became the Bruges Beurse and institutionalized their trading, the idea took off. It wasn't long before Ghent and Amsterdam, too, had their "Beurzen."

The concept spread through Europe. Bankers throughout Italy began to trade in government securities. In Holland joint stock companies were founded, and shareholders could invest and receive a share of profit or loss. In 1602, the first stocks and bonds were issued on the Amsterdam Stock Exchange by a company that played an important role around the globe and in the world of finance: the Dutch East India Company.

It was in Amsterdam, at the Beurs, that continuous trading began in the early 17th century. Innovative ways to trade were a hallmark of the period, and many of the speculative instruments still used today began on the Amsterdam Stock Exchange.

Today there are stock markets in nearly every developed country and in many developing countries.[1] Furthermore, in all manner of other kinds of financial markets, other securities, derivatives, bonds, and commodities can be traded. Who does this trading? Market participants run the gamut from gigantic aggregated groups to small, individual investors. They sit in luxurious offices in New York City skyscrapers and in kitchens in small towns, linked into the markets via personal computers. Many of their orders are taken and executed by professionals at the exchanges, but many others are done almost completely electronically on markets that are "virtual."

The roster of market participants represents a major change from the old days, when buyers and sellers were mostly wealthy businessmen. Today buyers and sellers are more likely to be institutions such as insurance companies, mutual funds, investor groups, banks, and pension funds. However, the opportunities for individual investors to "play the markets" have expanded along with the growth in the Internet and the World Wide Web.

Trades typically work like this: A potential buyer bids a specific price for a stock or whatever is being traded, and a potential seller asks a specific price. When there is a match, a sale takes place. Consider the case of a portfolio manager: He decides what a given portfolio ought to look like at any given time and thus what assets to invest in. He passes the order down to the buy-side trader, who implements the portfolio manager's objectives but in a manner that disguises to the market what the portfolio manager is actually trying to do. The buy-side trader passes the order to the broker, and finally the broker passes the order on to the exchange.

"That has been a pretty stable picture for quite a long time," says Dr. Benn Steil, "but I think we're going to be seeing some very

---

[1] The DMOZ Open Directory Project maintains a list that includes most of the "traditional," national-based stock exchanges throughout the world. See www.dmoz. org/Business/Investing/Stocks_and_Bonds/Exchanges//; accessed February 17, 2008.

significant change in the way this process works." Steil is a senior fellow and director of international economics at the Council on Foreign Relations. He is also one of the world's most recognized experts on financial markets and securities trading.

First, the exchange itself has undergone huge changes. Over the past 10 years, exchanges have been demutualizing—changing to shareholder-owned public companies. The effects have been massive. The exchanges have separated their ownerships and their memberships, also with major effects. The real revolution in exchange ownership and governance is affecting the relationship between the exchanges and the brokers.

COMPETITION

Now that the exchanges are themselves publicly listed companies, with a diversified shareholder base no longer controlled by the banks, they have become fierce competitors of banks. Furthermore, they have been exceptionally innovative in terms of introducing new products. One of the interesting effects over the past few years has been a major turnaround in the proportion of derivatives trading that happens on- rather than off-exchange. Though the OTC market is still much larger, the exchange-traded derivatives market has made major inroads. Indeed, even a big futures exchange such as the Chicago Mercantile Exchange is moving very aggressively into the OTC space.

One challenge brokers have faced is the pressure they come under from regulatory authorities. This is particularly the case with respect to the bundling that goes on in the trading process, where the buy side pays trading commissions that cover the cost of items unassociated with the trading process. Government scrutiny there, and on a number of other fronts, has increased, and margins in this intermediation area have been coming down significantly. Most of the challenges brokers face, however, come from the exchange side—from the organizations they once owned.

Increasingly, exchanges and brokers are competing. Traditionally, exchanges thought of brokers as their customers; in fact, their real customers are on the buy side. These are the institutional investors and, most important among them, the hedge funds—the most aggressive traders among the institutional investors. And why are they in competition? The brokers, by and large, bring orders from the hedge funds to the exchange. But the brokers are middlemen, and they take something in those transactions. As Steil sees it, "The exchanges are beginning to recognize that if they can cut out the middlemen like that, they can turn the costs of trading into revenue for themselves." To the extent that exchanges can cut unnecessary trading costs out of the process—costs that accrue not to others as revenue—the exchanges themselves can make money.

"This new picture," asks Steil, "with the portfolio manager giving the order to the buy-side trader, passing it on to the exchange—is this sort of the end of history? Is this where we are, is this where we end up?" His answer is that it probably is not, because "there are fascinating things going on on the buy side—important things that the exchanges have been ignoring at their peril."

SMART ORDER MANAGEMENT SYSTEMS

What are these important things the exchanges have been ignoring? To Steil, the most important is the growth of smart order management systems (OMS). "This has become a major part of the business on the buy side," Steil explains, "integrating order management and the execution process."

Recall how the traditional trading process works: The portfolio manager decides that he wants to take a large position—hundreds of thousands of shares, maybe millions of shares. He puts that into the OMS and communicates it to the buy-side trader. However, the buy-side trader does not reveal to the world that he wants to trade hundreds of thousands or even millions of shares. No; he chops it into very small pieces before he feeds it on to the exchange.

With smart OMS, the need for human intervention to disguise the order is beginning to fade. "There are two things going on within the order management system that I think are very important," says Steil. "First is the rise of algorithmic trading, which takes the human element entirely out of trading. Trading is increasingly dictated by computer programs—taking the buy-side trader out of the process. The second thing is actually much more threatening, not only to the buy-side trader but also to the exchange: New trading software being built into order management systems accommodates block trades, often called *dark pools*."

ALGORITHMIC TRADING

Electronic financial markets use computer programs to enter orders, with the computer algorithm deciding on many of the order aspects, including the price, timing, and sometimes the actual order quantity—hence the term *algorithmic trading*. This method can be used in any investment strategy, including arbitrage, market making, intermarket spreading, or even pure speculation. Decisions and implementation in these strategies can be completely automated, or the algorithmic support can be employed at any point along the way.

Algorithmic trading is used widely by institutional traders—in pension funds, mutual funds, hedge funds, and others—to manage the market impact, risk, and opportunity cost associated with their market activities. Management is achieved by dividing up a large trade into several smaller trades. Hedge funds and similar traders even use algorithmic trading to initiate orders based on information received electronically and possibly not even reviewed by human traders.

How prevalent is algorithmic trading? One estimate is that a third of all stock trades in the United States and the European Union were driven by automation in 2006. The figure is expected to reach 50 percent by 2010.[2]

The average order size on a traditional exchange system such as the New York Stock Exchange is about 400 shares. The average trade size on Liquidnet, enabled by OMS, is 42,000 shares. Liquidnet provides what it calls "seamless access to a global equities marketplace" for institutional

---

[2]Aite Group LLC, "Algorithmic Trading 2006: More Bells and Whistles," at www.aitegroup.com/reports/200610311.php; accessed February 25, 2008.

asset managers, making it possible for buy-side traders to "maintain complete control of their orders, executing anonymously, securely, and efficiently within the largest liquidity pools in the industry."[3]

According to Steil, "A system like Liquidnet knows what the portfolio manager wants to do, not what the buy-side trader chooses to tell the world."

Liquidnet, like other services of its kind, pulls all the OMSs from among its client base. If it finds a potential trading match, both sides are alerted, and, generally, they will do the block trade at the midpoint. This kind of automation, which is growing by leaps and bounds, is reducing trading costs significantly. In addition, smart OMS is reintegrating the trading process. "It is," explains Steil, "putting far more power in the hands of the portfolio manager, who in the future will need to be much more knowledgeable about trading processes and, in particular, how trading algorithms work."

There is a much larger issue, however, which Steil poses as a series of questions. "Are the exchanges not at risk that trading will evolve in such a manner that we see peer-to-peer trading? In other words, could the role of the exchange actually shrink as smart order management systems, not just within national marketplaces but across borders, increasingly communicate directly with each other and cut out the exchange?" The result would be to eliminate an important middleman.

This is the backdrop to a fascinating discussion of the future of the financial exchanges. In addition to OMS, demutualization is a fundamental part of the equation, and it is there that the discussion begins in earnest.

Demutualization

In the early 1990s, the Stockholm Stock Exchange faced a challenge: More and more trading in Swedish blue chip shares was finding its way to the London market. Smaller members of the Swedish Exchange did not want to have remote foreign members trading directly on the local exchange, so in 1993 Stockholm undertook a reform that gave rise to a revolution: It *demutualized.*

---

[3]www.liquidnet.com/cont/index/index.jsp; accessed January 14, 2008.

Demutualization is a process in which a stock exchange—or any member-owned mutual organization—changes to one that is owned by shareholders. A separate, logical follow-on step is to broaden the shareholder base by publicly listing the stock. That so many exchanges now do this is perhaps the most salient feature of the relentless pace of change intimated at earlier.

STOCKHOLM BEGINS THE PROCESS

Initially, the Stockholm Exchange separated ownership from membership by giving half the shares in the exchange to listed companies. When Optionsmäklama (OM) acquired the Stockholm Exchange in 1993, the latter became a listed company itself. What began in Stockholm has since resulted in a remarkable evolution of the marketplace.

To understand this evolution requires going back to the early 1980s, when Olof Stenhammar founded OM AB to introduce trading in standardized option contracts in Sweden. Regulation in Sweden at the time forbade running any exchanges other than the Stockholm Stock Exchange, so OM "disguised" itself as a broker. "From that platform," explains Per Larsson, "we gradually began to challenge the exchange's monopoly, which was abolished in 1989." Larsson, former OM group president, is today the chief executive officer of the Dubai International Financial Exchange.

OM acquired shares in the Stockholm Stock Exchange, eventually reaching a 20 percent ownership position. The Stockholm and Helsinki exchanges merged, and OMX—the new name of OM—began to embrace technology as a means to grow the business and innovate.

In essence, the entire demutualization movement began in the Nordic countries, spread south through Amsterdam into markets across the European continent, and found its way into London. Competition drove and continues to drive the process.

LONDON STOCK EXCHANGE

Founded in 1801, the London Stock Exchange (LSE) is one of the largest in the world. It traces its origins back even farther, to the coffeehouses of

17th-century London. In 1698, Jonathan's Coffee-house began to issue a list of stock and commodity prices; in the same year, Jonathan's and other coffeehouses became the sites for trading after stock dealers were expelled from the Royal Exchange for "rowdiness." Later, in 1761, a group of 150 brokers formed a club at Jonathan's to buy and sell shares, and eight years later the club built what came to be known as "The Stock Exchange"—a building with a dealing room on the ground floor and a coffee room upstairs. The modern stock exchange opened in 1801 with formal membership subscriptions.

In 2000, shareholders voted to become a public limited company, London Stock Exchange plc, and in 2001 the Exchange became a fully listed company on its own exchange. It is worth quoting from the London Stock Exchange's own Website to explain the rationale behind demutualization:

The global financial marketplace has become increasingly competitive and fast-moving. By becoming a for-profit commercial organization, the Exchange formally ended the link between membership and ownership. In doing so, we consolidated our position as a forward-thinking and powerful financial organization within the international capital markets.

And what does the Exchange see as the results? Through the process of demutualization, the LSE has developed "a clearer focus" on customer needs; "an improved and more effective approach to decision-making"; "flexibility" that allows the Exchange "to respond swiftly to changes in the international business arena"; "a fully commercial basis of operation"; and an understanding of shareholder needs.[4]

Martin Graham, director of market services for the London Stock Exchange, explains more specifically how demutualization has benefited the Exchange: "I think it's crucial to contrast the pre-demutualization situation to what we've achieved subsequently," says Graham. "Before demutualization, we had to manage the conflict between dissident client voices and sector interest groups. The quality of decision

[4]"London Stock Exchange: Demutualisation," at www.londonstockexchange.com/en-gb/products/consultancy/demutualisation.htm; accessed February 12, 2008.

making was, in some cases, poor, and we often ended up with decisions made by committees. For instance, the LSE made some information technology decisions that some have described as embarrassing failures."

Graham continues, "Some 99.9 percent of our members were in favor of demutualization. And now we run the market for the benefit of the entire market, which drives efficiency. For instance, we've seen average spreads reduced by 89 percent since demutualization, which has led to a massive increase in market efficiency. We have successfully invested in information technology to the extent that we are the first exchange to be launching new-generation trading technology. Since we've introduced SETS [the Stock Exchange Electronic Trading Service; see Chapter 2 for further description], we've seen trading in mid-caps increase by 250 percent, and the spread is down by 80 percent. In the pre-demutualized days, it would have been impossible to push that through, because sector interests that actually benefited from certain market inefficiencies would have been able to stop it."

From an overall structural and competition view, one benefit of demutualization is that it makes sense for stock exchanges to operate with the same essential rules and requirements under which investment banks and other players operate. For instance, demutualized exchanges must report to shareholders and respond to the same cost and other competitive pressures of the prevailing business environment. In addition, demutualization forces a kind of global architecture for financial exchanges that the mutual model did not support. Most business today must engage on the international playing field or at least needs some kind of international access. Demutualization opened the exchanges to shareholders around the world.

Another benefit has been in the area of metrics, especially those related to costs and efficiency. Mutual markets tended to be viewed as places for groups or firms or individual investors to come together and match trades, without any specific regard for how cost-efficient the process played out. Today, as corporate entities, the demutualized exchanges not only must but do evaluate efficiency. The process is still in its infancy, and consistency across exchanges with respect to the metrics has not been achieved, but the availability of data and increasing consistency have helped make benchmarking a closer reality.

DEMUTUALIZED EXCHANGES

Though it's by no means an exhaustive list, here are the principal exchanges that have demutualized, beginning in 1993:

Stockholm Stock Exchange (1993)	Stock Exchange of Singapore (2000)
Helsinki Stock Exchange (1995)	Hong Kong Stock Exchange (2000)
Copenhagen Stock Exchange (1996)	Toronto Stock Exchange (2000)
Amsterdam Stock Exchange (1997)	London Stock Exchange (2000)
Borsa Italiana (1997)	Deutsche Börse (2000)
Australian Stock Exchange (1998)	Euronext (2000)
Iceland Stock Exchange (1999)	Nasdaq (2000)
Simex (1999)	New York Mercantile Exchange (2000)
Athens Stock Exchange (1999)	Chicago Mercantile Exchange (2002)

As Martin Graham sees it, "Demutualization has been a massive benefit to the entire market. It has enabled us to actually create huge market growth and efficiency for the benefit of the entire market."

NYMEX

Some demutualization processes have been undertaken in steps rather than through wholesale transformation. The New York Mercantile Exchange (NYMEX) is a case in point. The exchange traces its origins to the 1872 establishment of a marketplace in New York City for trading dairy products. Ten years later, when trade expanded to dried fruits, canned goods, and poultry, the New York Mercantile Exchange name was adopted. Further expansion came when NYMEX merged in 1994 with the New York Commodities Exchange (COMEX), which had been established in 1933 through the merger of exchanges devoted to metals, rubber, raw silk, and hides. Today, NYMEX is the world's largest physical commodity futures exchange.

For most of its history, NYMEX was a mutual organization, and trading took place exclusively on the floor of its headquarters. The New York exchange even expanded this model to London, opening a trading floor there. Then it began a path to demutualization.

In the late 1990s and early part of this century, NYMEX began to bring in some private equity money to help fund its expansion. This move coincided with a decision by the exchange leadership to move toward becoming a publicly traded company. The question, says NYMEX Chief Executive Officer Jim Newsome, was how to best do so.

"We needed a catalyst to help us drive that change," Newsome explains. "Given our old governance structure, we determined it was going to be very difficult to move in that direction on a timely basis without a catalyst to help us do so. So we went with the world's largest private equity firms—for which we took some criticism. I think some felt like we were conducting an auction, looking for the highest bidder. But that was not our goal at all. We were looking for a partner."

NYMEX used the vote of its members on entering an agreement with a private equity firm to drive the governance and membership changes needed to move forward toward becoming a public company. "It allowed us," recalls Newsome, "to move very quickly. We made the governance changes and put more authority in the hands of a smaller, more pro-business board. We knew exactly what changes had to be made, and we implemented them fast."

In the case of NYMEX, the competitive environment helped induce members to move more quickly than they might have done otherwise, especially competition from the Intercontinental Exchange (ICE), which operates global commodity and financial products marketplaces and has one of the most advanced electronic trading platforms in the world. It was, according to Newsome, "an example of competition driving positive change, which benefited the sector."

ISE

Not all publicly traded exchanges went through a process of demutualization. Some began their lives as publicly traded companies. The International Securities Exchange (ISE), for example, launched in 2000 without having to go through the process of demutualizing an old mutualized exchange. ISE "operates a family of fully electronic trading platforms" and its markets portfolio "consists of an options exchange and a stock exchange." It is the "world's largest equity options trading venue."[5]

David Krell is ISE's chief executive officer. "Change is hard, particularly in the financial services industry," says Krell, "We were trying to drive change. We were trying to create a more automated marketplace, a fully electronic marketplace that we introduced in the options business in the United States. But we did much more than that. We created an entirely different market structure."

EURONEXT

Demutualization of the financial exchanges has also driven mergers, often the same kinds of megamergers typically seen in other industries. On the European continent, the process has been accompanied by a series of exchange mergers that have profoundly shaped the landscape. Euronext offers an ideal example. In September 2000, the Amsterdam Stock Exchange, Brussels Stock Exchange, and Paris Bourse effected a merger to take advantage of the harmonization of financial markets within the European Union. Euronext was born, and by 2006 it was NYSE Euronext, formed from the merger of the New York Stock Exchange, Euronext, and NYSE Arca. Today NYSE Euronext operates a family of exchanges in six countries.

Olivier Lefebvre, a member of the NYSE Euronext managing committee, explains the types of conflicting objectives that demutualization has helped address. "I joined the Brussels Stock Exchange in 1996, when it

---

[5]"About ISE," at www.ise.com/WebForm/viewPage.aspx?categoryId=105&header5=true; accessed February 12, 2008.

was a not-for-profit mutual owned by the banks and the brokers. At the time, I was prohibited from going to London to attract new members. That illustrates precisely the sort of difficulties with a mutual, which works fine as long as you are in a monopolistic situation. But in a competitive world where trading has moved from the exchange floor to computers, where you can have remote members, and where members can play on several exchanges, the problems begin. I believe that is why all markets changed their governance systems."

Euronext's innovation was to embrace fully the notion of trading via information technology and deliver a fully integrated market by combining various regulated markets without destroying what Lefebvre calls their "home value." This is essential to Euronext's objective as fully electronic exchanges that produce liquidity. Consolidation and information technology, in a demutualization context, make it possible to meet that objective.

The potential for more exchange mergers certainly exists, although the big financial institutions are not always ready to embrace any merger that comes along. As with mergers between large industrial firms, investment banks are asking where the benefits will come in and what the potential costs might be. As one senior executive at a major investment bank puts it, a lot of people don't understand exchanges as businesses, and consolidation of exchanges is forcing some issues that need to be forced but also provoking people to wonder whether consolidation is the most efficient step to take. The issues range from cross-border regulation to the ability of technologies to accommodate trading across asset classes.

DTCC

To be sure, some firms ancillary to the exchanges have found demutualization not to be to their benefit. Consider the Depository Trust & Clearing Corporation (DTCC), created in response to the paperwork crisis that developed in the securities industry in the late 1960s and 1970s. New York Stock Exchange brokers used to exchange paper certificates and checks for each of its millions of daily trades, and Wall Street was awash with hundreds of messengers rushing about to make the deliveries.

Donald Donahue, the chief executive officer of DTCC, explains that his firm is industry owned. "We actually remutualized," says Donahue, "when everyone else was in the throes of demutualizing. We actually altered our ownership structure and forced all of our members to buy stock in DTCC—something they had been offered in the past but that had not been a requirement."

Every industry goes through cycles, and it may well be that the exchange industry as a whole will see a cycle of demutualization and remutualization. "It is a very natural part of industries that operate in a competitive environment," explains Philip Hylander, global head of equities trading for Goldman Sachs. "If you will, it is the cost of there being competition. There is, of course, another option: heavy regulation, with price controls. But we need innovation, too. So, are you prepared to tolerate the cycle of competition, the fragmentation and then reconsolidation, in order to get the benefits both in price and in quality of service? We vote yes."

Demutualization, and the potential cycle of remutualization, brings the financial exchanges into the company of other industries. It is how industry builds when there is competition.

The evidence points to improved transparency of markets, increased investment, and enhanced overall quality in the world of demutualized financial exchanges. The jury is still out as to whether these outcomes can be linked directly to public ownership; after all, pressure from shareholders is not always the reason a publicly traded company functions better. But there is little denying that it is since demutualization that most exchanges have seen greater attention paid to market quality. With demutualization, exchanges have also gained more independence from the smaller group of selling-side owners and now enjoy the benefit of shareholder opinions from the selling side.

Ruben Lee, chairman of Oxford Finance Group, offers a good summary of the merits of demutualization: "More responsive to customers, more flexible governance, currency for mergers and acquisition. You can unlock members' equity, reward market participants, get access to capital, and improve financial decision making."

Lee asks, "Do demutualized exchanges deliver value? Of course they do. If we look at the rates of return earned by the demutualized exchanges since 1993, pretty much all of them have earned very high rates of return relative, on a consistent basis, to almost all other industries. Why do demutualized, listed exchanges deliver value? They have innovated. They have focused on clients. They have delivered new products."

The demutualization movement poses the question of whether it is even possible today to operate a major international exchange as a mutual organization. Andreas Preuss, chief executive officer of Eurex, thinks the answer will soon be no.

EUREX

Eurex is one of the world's largest derivative exchanges and Europe's leading clearinghouse. It is jointly operated by Deutsche Börse AG and SWX Swiss Exchange. In December 2007, Eurex completed the acquisition of ISE, which is now a wholly owned subsidiary of Eurex. Together, Eurex and ISE comprise "the global market leader in individual equity and equity index derivatives."[6]

Preuss says that mutual organizations need to accept their "upcoming demise." Why? "Mutual exchange organizations have fundamental disadvantages compared to demutualized exchange organizations," he explains. For example, speed will become increasingly important, and the desire for incessant technology improvements is much stronger in a demutualized environment. It is probably most developed in an environment of publicly listed companies that are focused on fulfilling the legitimate expectations of the entire spectrum of stakeholders— and certainly among them shareholders hold a very prominent position.

Just how strong is this trend toward demutualization? One of Eurex's operating partners, SWX Swiss Exchange, remains a mutual organization. Yet Preuss does not believe that it gets in the way of organizational decision making at Eurex. The competitive environment trumps whatever tendency the mutual organization might have to make business decisions appropriate to a different model.

We are not even two full decades into the era of financial exchange demutualization. It might not be too long before every exchange or at least all the major global exchanges shift to a profit-oriented structure

---

[6]"Eurex: About Us," at www.eurexchange.com/about_en.html; accessed February 12, 2008.

and public trading of ownership shares. As the process unfolds, many issues have come to the fore. Some are unique to the demutualization of financial exchanges, and some have been faced by other industries. One of the key issues in the latter category is governance.

Corporate Governance

The governance of market infrastructure institutions—the exchanges themselves as well as a settlement system such as a central counterparty (CCP) clearinghouse or central securities depository (CSD)—has become a pressing issue as corporate governance overall continues to fill the business press. It is an area that, unfortunately, is lacking in some clarity in what is widely acknowledged to be a difficult environment.

What are the fundamental questions? The first is: What *is* governance? Broadly speaking, governance is about power: who has it, how they get it, why they get it, and how and why they use it. That power exists in many different configurations. With respect to ownership, it includes several formal structures: board committee appointments, voting rights, regulation, and management. But it is also informal. For instance, customers have power in a competitive market. They can choose to take their business elsewhere. So, too, do suppliers have power. There are others with power, depending on the types of relationships they have with the marketplace. Lawyers and lenders are examples. The market also has its own power.

Politics, which expresses public power, plays a role as well. Political intervention is growing in markets. Ruben Lee, chairman of Oxford Finance Group, identifies three reasons. "First," he says, "to the extent that there is competition and vested interests don't like it and they find it difficult to compete, they will look to political jurisdictions or interests to protect their money."

The second reason has to do with the consolidation of trading. "As trading consolidates," says Lee, "it brings power to the biggest institutions. For instance, the New York Stock Exchange is not simply a market; it is a very political institution, as indeed are most of the major markets. There's no escaping that a major exchange plays a role in a nation."

The third reason is self-evident, as Lee sees it. "To the extent that we have international stuff going on," he explains, "then once again we have interests between different types of nations."

All this plays out in the context of the private *and* public goods provided by exchanges, CCPs, and CSDs. Lee wonders whether the governance of these infrastructure institutions matters.

"The first answer is no," says Lee. "What matters are the decisions they take. What concerns us are outcomes." Why, then, is there such a raging debate about governance?

The first reason has to do with the effectiveness of various governance structures. Then there are concerns that governance affects regulatory outcomes. In a demutualized environment, there is the ongoing question of conflicts of interest. There has been a range of governance problems at institutions that led to dramatic changes in leadership at the New York Stock Exchange, for example, as well as at Deutsche Börse. Whether or not one views the exchanges as corporations, it is the general focus on *corporate* governance has brought attention to the governance of demutualized institutions.

FURTHER DEFINITIONS OF CORPORATE GOVERNANCE

The online "Encyclopedia About Corporate Governance"[7] could not be more correct when it states that the concept of corporate governance tends to be poorly defined. Because it "potentially covers a large number of distinct economic phenomenon," notes the encyclopedia, "different people have come up with different definitions that basically reflect their special interest in the field." To help facilitate some order among this disorder, the encyclopedia lists some of these differing definitions. We offer a smaller selection here:

From the Organization for Economic Cooperation and Development, we read: "Corporate governance is the system by which business corporations are directed and controlled. The corporate governance structure specifies the distribution of rights and responsibilities among different participants in the corporation, such as the board, managers, shareholders and other stakeholders, and spells out the rules and procedures for making decisions

---

[7]www.encycogov.com/WhatIsGorpGov.asp; accessed June 13, 2008.

on corporate affairs. By doing this, it also provides the structure through which the company objectives are set, and the means of attaining those objectives and monitoring performance."[8]

The World Bank offers this definition: "Corporate governance is about promoting corporate fairness, transparency and accountability."[9]

A more cynical definition reads, "Corporate governance deals with the ways in which suppliers of finance to corporations assure themselves of getting a return on their investment."[10]

And finally: "Some commentators take too narrow a view, and say it (corporate governance) is the fancy term for the way in which directors and auditors handle their responsibilities toward shareholders. Others use the expression as if it were synonymous with shareholder democracy. Corporate governance is a topic recently conceived, as yet ill-defined, and consequently blurred at the edges . . . corporate governance as a subject, as an objective, or as a regime to be followed for the good of shareholders, employees, customers, bankers and indeed for the reputation and standing of our nation and its economy."[11]

The merits of demutualization have been established. Further, the question of whether the demutualized exchanges deliver value has also been answered—with a *yes*. The rates of return since 1993 have been consistently quite high relative to all other industries. The demutualized exchanges have innovated, focused on clients, and delivered new markets and new products. They have also posed new governance questions.

---

[8]OECD, April 1999.

[9]James D. Wolfensohn, president of the Word Bank, as quoted in an article in *Financial Times*, June 21, 1999.

[10]Andrei Shleifer and Robert W. Vishny, "A Survey of Corporate Governance," *The Journal of Finance* 52:2 (June 1997), p. 737.

[11]N. G. Maw, L. Horsell, and M. Craig-Cooper, *Maw on Corporate Governance*, Cambridge, England: Cambridge University Press, 1994, p. 1.

Governance and the Issue of Market Power

"Wherever the demutualized exchanges have found it possible to exploit market power, they have done so," says Lee. "And standard corporate governance responses won't solve the problem. On the contrary, they will exacerbate it." Standard corporate governance responses aim to ensure that management looks after the interest of shareholders to solve the principle-agent problem—that is, the conflict that arises when people (agents) entrusted to look after the interests of others (principals) use their power to benefit themselves instead. In the case of demutualized exchanges, the issue comes up in the competing contexts of competition and monopoly. That is why the question of whether exchanges have market power is so important.

What is the answer to that question? There are lots of signs that competition is alive and well and that exchanges *do not* have market power. For instance, there are various trading systems reflecting the different ways in which people like to trade. That implies competition. Internalization—that is, the execution of customer trades by financial intermediaries, off the primary market—allows brokers to compete with the exchanges. Automation has allowed the creation of new systems. Disintermediation has spelled the removal of the middleman from many transactions. Smart order routing facilitates the breaking of the network externality—that is, the situation in which the price someone is willing to pay to gain access to a network is based only on how many other people are using that network.

There are, though, some restrictions on competition—at least in the view of some observers. An important one is size. When exchanges merge and realize deep economies of scale, does competition suffer? And do we really have competition when the largest exchanges still have such a significant percentage of market share?

Even if an exchange had 100 percent market share, it would not automatically mean that the exchange could exercise market power. It all depends on whether the threshold for potential competition to enter the fray is low enough. But new entrants do not automatically mean the end to market power, if it exists.

The question of whether the exchanges have market power is also relevant to CCPs and CSDs, where user governance is largely present.

This type of governance corresponds to the reality of CCPs and CSDs. First, they are established for the users, and the users can force the institution to deliver what they want. The users, in this sense, represent the public interest. Further, user governance is a buffer against monopolistic activity. If a CCP decides to maximize profits by raising prices, users— who are the owners—will likely rebel. They will demand that they be charged competitive prices.

WHY MARKET POWER IS A CONCERN

Economists define "market power" as the ability of a firm to alter the market price of a good or service. In other words, having market power means that you can raise a price without worrying that your customers will go to your competitors. You can also manipulate the quantity of goods or services available in the market. The behaviors exhibited when market power exists are unilateral and anticompetitive. This is why many countries have enacted legislation (such as antitrust laws) aimed at limiting firms' ability to accrue market power.

But is user governance desirable? The answer begins with looking at what users are required to do and are responsible for as directors and how they actually operate.

Users have a fiduciary duty to the institutions on whose boards they sit, which means that they wear two hats. Obviously that is a fine arrangement when the interests coincide, but it raises issues when they do not. Users also have a responsibility with respect to confidentiality. Often the people who sit on boards do not know much about the very issues that they must examine, and so they must get expert opinions. Often the experts reside at a director's own firm. If that director is required to keep everything in that institution confidential, it becomes nearly impossible to share the internal information necessary to get the needed expertise.

It is impossible for a board to have full representation of all its users. That leads institutions to employ different types of "equations" to determine who should be represented—and often to homogeneous boards, which some empirical evidence suggests function well but also lead to homogeneous markets. Representation decisions must also consider the issue of having "independent" directors, which is being required more and more by regulators. But who is independent? Do these potential board members have any relevant knowledge?

The bottom-line question is whether governance is even relevant. It certainly is in the context of one of the most intriguing issues facing the business world in general: socially responsible investing.

GOVERNANCE AND SOCIALLY RESPONSIBLE INVESTING

Responsible corporate behavior and responsible investing have never been more relevant than they are today. We see activity in these areas on the buy side and among companies. More recently, there is more attention to these issues on the sell side and among analysts. To a certain degree, the exchanges themselves are taking up these concerns.

What are the buy side, sell side, and exchanges doing, and what should they be doing? Emma Hunt is a senior associate with Mercer Investment Consulting, based in London, where she supports clients on issues relating to responsible investment and shareholder engagement. Prior to joining Mercer, she spent two years at the Forum for the Future, which describes itself as a "charity committed to sustainable development." There, Hunt headed up the Centre for Sustainable Investment, which was set up "to help build capacity in the financial services sector."[12]

Hunt has noticed a significant shift in attitudes and levels of knowledge about what she prefers to call "responsible investment." She attributes this shift to several developments. One is greater sophistication in the understanding of corporate governance, with a new willingness to venture into engagement as a way to protect or add value within a portfolio. This links to the underlying principles of corporate governance, including transparency.

Even pension funds are changing their behavior. "We're seeing some funds take a more active interest in their fund managers' voting and engagement reports," reports Hunt. "Some are even taking their voting in-house because they want to retain that responsibility."

[12]www.forumforthefuture.org; accessed February 16, 2008.

The greater understanding of what responsible investment *is* also has a major effect. The old definition has been expanded well beyond simple ethical screening. "Today there is a recognition that this is more about integrating environmental, social, and corporate governance factors into the investment process," says Hunt, "where these are material to company performance."

Globalization—in its many facets—is helping to drive the change. Says Hunt, "We're seeing large pension funds and companies themselves beginning to recognize we're living in a very different global business environment. We've got a much stronger global media network. We have greater environmental regulations, social regulation, voluntary codes, and so on. All of this makes these traditionally nonfinancial issues have a much stronger impact on company performance and, therefore, investment performance."

INDUSTRY INITIATIVES AND VOLUNTARY CODES

Industry initiatives and voluntary codes have also expanded. This reflects both government trepidation over using regulation to control markets and the market players themselves demanding that they be left alone. Among many other initiatives are institutional shareholder committee codes of practice, popular in the United Kingdom; the King's Code of Corporate Governance in South Africa; the guidelines established by the Association of British Insurers; and so on. "These industry initiatives," says Hunt, "have extended to responsible investment and have gone a long way to promoting these underlying principles. They are not something regulators are giving us."

At the United Nations, 20 of the world's largest investors, mainly pension funds but also some charitable investors and an insurance company, came together to develop the Principles for Responsible Investment (PRI), a framework for investment professionals to consider the "environmental, social and corporate governance (ESG) issues [that] can affect the performance of investment portfolios."[13] The principles

---

[13]"About the Principles for Responsible Investment," at www.unpri.org/about/; accessed February 16, 2008.

are supported by about 200 asset owners, investment managers, and professional service partners who have become signatories, and that number is growing.[14] These signatories represent more than $8 trillion in assets.

Stock exchanges can play an important role in encouraging these types of voluntary codes and sets of principles. But are these voluntary codes enough? Should there be changes in listings requirements? Do regulators need to be given more responsibility in this area, despite the reaction of the business community to regulation?

"Voluntary codes are only as strong as the monitoring measurement reporting that goes with them," explains Hunt. The U.N. PRI has a commitment to reporting, and there is an important assessment process for all signatories.

There is also a cultural issue. Voluntary codes work in some places but probably not in others. For instance, the United Kingdom has a legal system based on case law and discussion and negotiation, and so voluntary codes have worked well in that environment. In the Netherlands, where a civil code is the basis for law, there is great familiarity with the concept of making something happen in practice that is based on high-level principles. In France and Germany, the cultural environment is much more rule-driven, and so voluntary codes will not necessary work. More likely, laws need to be written in those countries.

In the case of the U.N. Principles for Responsible Investment, no regulators or exchanges have become signatories. It may well be that today's demutalized exchanges have other concerns and priorities, despite the fact that the United Nations and others suggested five or six years ago that the exchanges would move to establish these sorts of principles into their own listing rules. Of course, in the case of the European Union, a directive or regulation takes at least five years to be established; some have taken upward of four decades. Changes, assuming everyone is in agreement, take three years. The compliance process takes another seven years.

Michelle Edkins is managing director at Governance for Owners, an independent partnership among major financial institutions, shareowners,

---

[14]"Signatories to the Principles for Responsible Investment," at www.unpri.org/signatories/#im; accessed February 16, 2008.

and executives, and was previously the head of the corporate governance team at Hermes Pension Management. "In terms of enforcement," says Edkins, "most voluntary codes in the area of corporate governance are structured such that the onus is on the shareholders to make sure that the companies they invest in meet their expectations on best practice."

Exchanges must have a strong understanding of corporate governance if they want to support good practices by the issuers who are on their exchanges. "In my opinion," says Edkins, "corporate governance is about three things: quality of leadership, transparency, and accountability." All three of these apply to exchanges, just as they apply to other corporations.

"Quality of leadership," explains Edkins, "means having a board and a team of senior executives that are well qualified for the job, with experience, interest, and talent. Bringing that together and making it work well is why corporate governance drives performance, why good standards of corporate governance, good standards of leadership, or high-quality leadership influences organizational performance. It is common sense: A company headed by strong, capable, well-informed people is more likely to be able to deliver what investors want—long-term, sustainable performance—and more likely to be able to deal with the issues of managing a business that sometimes trip businesses up."

TRANSPARENCY

Transparency, for Edkins, is about communicating with all the parties that have a legitimate interest in the business. That includes people who have invested in, work for, or rely on the business or who supply the business with goods and services. Open communication makes it possible for people who participate or interact with a business to do so with sound knowledge of what the business is involved in and what the risks might be.

In the corporate model, this includes shareholders. They can appoint and remove members of the board of directors and need to have directors who operate in their long-term interests. "Investors have a central role to play in overseeing boards and creating a dynamic link in the corporate governance chain," says Edkins. "Otherwise corporate governance operates in a vacuum and is relatively meaningless." To be responsible owners, investors must vote intelligently at the general meeting. They must communicate their views and give directors and management an opportunity to react.

One specific role that exchanges and the sell side can play involves providing a standard of best practice. "I really do believe," says Edkins, "that a high level of corporate governance in a market is a sign of quality of investment." This is something about which exchanges should be particularly concerned. Beyond that, exchanges can be proactive in taking steps to ensure that their reputations are not undermined. For instance, foreign companies taking listings on certain exchanges might not be required to adopt standards of best practice—and that fact might not be well known by investors. Exchanges can address this concern. Sell-side firms have an important role to play by incorporating quality-of-management assessments into their analysis of companies. The more they can look at some of the "extra-financial" issues, the more they facilitate better decision making.

Edkins recounts that the chief financial officer of a major European-listed company told her that his company looks very closely at these sorts of issues. "Some people say these issues are esoteric," she explains, "but he said these are the things that can jeopardize his business. And even if they don't initially start out as having financial criteria, they nearly always do in the long term."

The strong global interest in corporate governance practices and responsible investing begs the question of why there is still any resistance to stock exchanges addressing these issues. After all, as businesses that have demutualized and that are themselves listed, shouldn't they be stepping up to the plate like any other corporate citizen would be expected to do?

The fact is that more and more exchanges are addressing these issues. The London Stock Exchange collects and publishes information on the corporate and social activity of companies it lists but depends on those companies for the information. There is a compelling case for the stock exchanges to do this and more, especially when they are competing to become the favored listing group for an emerging market company. And there is a compelling case for the exchanges to have high standards expressed through their listing requirements. The future promises even more attention to corporate governance and responsible investing.

But what about regulation?

Regulation Today

Few exchange executives *enjoy* being regulated, but nearly all recognize regulation as a necessary part of business. The regulators themselves face enormous challenges, especially in a world where markets are increasingly international. They must keep up with what is happening in the real world, and today they are doing things that they probably would not have dreamed of doing even a mere five years ago.

In the United States, for instance, regulation itself faces increased scrutiny. As Mary Schapiro, former chairman and chief executive officer of the National Association of Securities Dealers (NASD), explains, "There is a raging debate in the United States about the competitiveness of U.S. markets and whether New York is losing its preeminence as the world's financial center to London or Hong Kong or other financial centers."

THE COMPETITIVENESS DEBATE

From Schapiro's perspective, the debate was crystallized in part by three major reports released in 2006 and 2007: one from the U.S. Chamber of Commerce; another by a U.S. House of Representatives committee; and the third from U.S. Senator Charles Schumer (Dem.-New York) and New York City Mayor Michael Bloomberg. The reports raise questions not only about New York's loss of preeminence but also about the status of the Chicago Mercantile Exchange. They point not only to the regulatory regimes but also to the private litigation environment in the United States—especially what has happened in the wake of the Sarbanes-Oxley Act of 2002. This legislation introduced major changes to the regulation of corporate governance and financial practice, and—most controversially—established an overarching public company accounting board.[15]

Is the regulatory regime the cause of New York's decline? Is New York's decline real? Mary Schapiro sees what has happened as part and parcel of an increasingly complex financial services market. "What has

---

[15]Public Company Accounting Reform and Investor Protection Act of 2002, Pub.L. 107-204, 116 Stat. 745, enacted July 30, 2002.

happened is that globalization is taking hold and, as you would naturally expect, other financial centers around the world are becoming more prominent. Markets have matured, economies have matured, and it is a perfectly natural result that London, Hong Kong, Paris, and other markets have begun to become more equal with New York."

Though disputing that regulation itself is the culprit, Schapiro acknowledges that globalization requires adopting a new perspective. "It really has forced us to look carefully at our regulatory structure. What can we do to be more sensitive to these issues?" she asks. "How can we streamline the process of being a regulated entity in the United States, particularly for our companies that have a global presence?"

The 200 largest broker-dealers in the world are also members of the New York Stock Exchange, which means that they must abide two sets of examinations, follow two sets of rules that sometimes conflict, deal with two sets of enforcement staffs, participate in two arbitration forums, and so on. So NASD's response set out to engage the NYSE in discussions about consolidating regulatory operations, beginning in July 2006. The result was the July 2007 launch of the Financial Industry Regulatory Authority (FINRA). It is, according to Schapiro, "a small but important piece of streamlining the regulatory spaghetti bowl that we have in the United States."

FINRA

FINRA is the largest nongovernmental regulatory body for all securities firms doing business in the United States, created through the consolidation of NASD and the member regulation, enforcement, and arbitration functions of NYSE. It oversees close to 5,000 brokerage firms, about 172,000 branch offices, and more than 676,000 registered securities representatives.[16] Mary Schapiro is now FINRA's chief executive officer.

"The creation of FINRA is the most significant modernization of the self-regulatory regime in decades," Schapiro explains on the FINRA

---

[16]"About the Financial Industry Regulatory Authority," at www.finra.org/AboutFINRA/index.htm; accessed March 7, 2008.

Website. "With investor protection and market integrity as our over-arching objectives, FINRA is an investor-focused and more streamlined regulator that is better suited to the complexity and competitiveness of today's global capital markets."[17]

FINRA addresses some of the regulatory challenges faced in the United States. But what about the regulatory picture in other countries, where markets and the participants may be quite different? Walter Lukken, acting chairman of the U.S. Commodity Futures Trading Commission (CFTC), is concerned with globalization of futures markets. "Globalization," explains Lukken, has caused competition to become borderless."

In 1986, CFTC developed a system for firms that now allows foreign exchanges to place terminals in the United States as long as the exchanges are subject to a comparable regulatory structure.[18] "The whole idea," Lukken says, "was to try and create some type of seamless regulatory fabric around the world—not necessarily because regulators wanted to do this but because the industry needed it. We have to reflect what the industry looks like. We just came to this juncture sooner than the securities markets did, but now they are there."

Today the U.S. Securities and Exchange Commission (SEC) is facing the same question CFTC confronted years back: how to create a structure that allows regulation to cover foreign firms without hindering business operations or market structure. The SEC appears to be following roughly the same path as the CFTC. Further, the SEC is engaged in more dialogue with European regulatory authorities. Generally, says Lukken, there is recognition that "market structures have to be structured across borders."

THE SEC: ONE STORY OF REGULATION

In 1934, the U.S. Congress established the Securities and Exchange Commission as an independent, nonpartisan, quasijudicial regulatory agency. The legislators recognized that in the wake of the stock market crash of 1929 and the Great Depression that followed, there needed to be some way

Continued

---

[17]*Ibid.*
[18]17 CFR Part 30, "Foreign Futures and Foreign Options Transactions."

THE SEC: ONE STORY OF REGULATION—Continued

to regulate the stock market and prevent corporate abuses relating to the offering and sale of securities and corporate reporting. The SEC was given the power to license and regulate stock exchanges. It was, in the SEC's own words, "an era ripe for reform."

Over the years, the SEC has taken on the responsibility of administering six major U.S. laws that govern the securities industry. Congress gave the SEC authority to enforce these laws and bring civil actions against companies or individuals who commit accounting fraud, engage in insider trading, provide false information, or violate securities law in other ways. The SEC also works with law enforcement agencies when these violations warrant criminal prosecution.

Today the SEC defines its mission this way: "to protect investors, maintain fair, orderly, and efficient markets, and facilitate capital formation.... And the common interest of all Americans in a growing economy that produces jobs, improves our standard of living, and protects the value of our savings means that all of the SEC's actions must be taken with an eye toward promoting the capital formation that is necessary to sustain economic growth."[19]

CESR

The big regulatory challenge in Europe involves Euronext. The Committee of European Securities Regulators (CESR) is responsible for meeting the challenge, which is multifaceted. First, there remain big differences from one country to the next in Europe, and the political situations can be quite diverse. The European Commission has issued many directives that speak to financial market issues across country lines,

---

[19]"The Investor's Advocate: How the SEC Protects Investors, Maintains Market Integrity, and Facilitates Capital Formation," at www.sec.gov/about/whatwedo.shtml; accessed April 11, 2008.

many of which are designed to make investment in Europe more attractive to the rest of the world. That is where CESR comes in.

CESR was established by a 2001 European Commission decision to improve coordination among securities regulators within the European Union countries; advise the Commission; and work to ensure more consistent and timely day-to-day implementation of European Community legislation within the member countries.[20] Among other issues, CESR's technical advisors and working groups address gaps between U.S. and European regulations. Within Europe itself, though, the question remains of whether there should be one regulator for all countries of the European Union and, if so, how practical that might be.

It is a daunting issue because regulation has become a key driver of competition, not only between marketplaces but also between countries and their economies. That is why many see the CFTC and European regulators' decision to allow each other's exchanges to place trading screens in each other's countries has not only been a benefit to the buyer side of the market equation but also an overall economic benefit. The reason? It has created greater market liquidity, specifically in the bond markets, which in turn has resulted in lower debt and capital financing. Since the decision to allow trading screens from one country to be placed in another was a decision taken by multiple regulators, some would argue that it shows that having different regulators is generally good for the market and establishes a kind of "sanity check" across borders.

The question of one versus many regulators has yet to be resolved. For instance, the cornerstone of the European Commission's Financial Services Action Plan, created in 1999, is the Markets in Financial Instruments Directive (MiFID), aimed at harmonizing the regulatory regime for investment services across all 27 member states of the European Union along with Norway, Iceland, and Liechtenstein. Some have suggested that it establishes a *de facto* single regulator in Europe. Others see its value in making it possible to exchange information among regulators in different countries. Still others wonder whether MiFID is reducing the cost of capital—which they see as the key to measuring its result.

---

[20]Committee of European Securities Regulators, "About Us," at www.cesr-eu.org/index.php?page=cesrinshort&mac=0&id=; accessed March 7, 2008.

The need to satisfy multiple regulators can create a great deal of problems. A steel company that has listings on three different exchanges must deliver its completed disclosure to all three exchanges and three different regulators with different requirements in terms of what is reported. A company listed in Germany, for instance, is required to record the date of birth of all shareholders. In the United States, that is information one would be hard-pressed to extract from shareholders.

Mary Schapiro would like, at minimum, to see more convergence between what U.S. and European regulators seek from issuers. "One plea I hear frequently is for regulators to harmonize their information requests to regulated firms so that when we're asking you for data in a particular context, our request doesn't look different than what the U.K. regulators or those in Amsterdam ask for. Firms spend fortunes building systems that are generating the data, and if everybody has a little bit different way they want that data because they're used to using it a particular way, it adds enormous cost."

Of course, the absence of a single lead regulator also leaves open the possibility of overlap between various regulatory bodies—and that can lead to disputes ending up in the courts. One market executive suggests that making a clear distinction between *principles* and *regulations* is a good way to head off those sorts of problems. For instance, at the level of principles, the Financial Services Authority in the United Kingdom—the independent body that regulates the financial services industry, with a wide range of rule-making, investigatory, and enforcement powers—might engage its counterpart in the Netherlands to discuss key issues. For instance, they might debate the nature of today's market failures and how they might evolve. From those discussions, principles might emerge to guide policy making. But from a regulatory perspective, the economic and industry structures as well as the legal frameworks from one country to the next might be so different as to make a one-size-fits-all approach not only difficult but potentially dangerous. For this reason, many experts advise focusing on market outcomes, which depend on *context* that is likely to be country-specific.

In the United States, the discussion of principle-based regulation continues to unfold. In Europe, stacks of rules seem to be increasingly replacing principle-based regulation. As Luis Correia da Silva sees it, the main issue is the competitiveness of the regulatory framework. Correia da Silva is the managing director and joint CEO of Oxford

Economic Research Associates (Oxera), an independent economics consultancy established in 1982. He sees the U.K/European regulatory regime—still more principle based than in the United States—as having a great number of advantages.

"It is more prone to innovation," says Correia da Silva, "and in the United Kingdom the regulatory regime allows for new products to come into the market. It also has the advantage that it allows us to think the market outcomes we want to improve, whereas rules-based regulation is much more about the inputs into the process. It is very difficult to go from the rule all the way to the market outcome that that rule is supposed to be improving."

Still, even Correia da Silva will admit that rules-based regulation has its own advantage. "It minimizes regulatory uncertainty," he explains. "So I think there are pros and cons, but I still think principle-based regulation, given the nature of capital markets, is the right way forward. We must, though, make sure we define precisely what we mean by principles-based."

GLOBAL CONSIDERATIONS

Whatever the direction, there need to be global considerations. As Mary Schapiro sees it, "Maybe we've been slow to the realization that we have to join the rest of the world and deal with our issues on a far more global and less domestic basis than we have historically. Regulators really have been forced by the business moving ahead. It doesn't work for regulators to play catch-up or put in place the perfect system for, say, a transatlantic exchange merger. We need to be constructive players in the discussion and debate and not just try to stop people at the door. If we're going to be modern regulators, we have to take notice of changes and understand and work with our industry to accomplish them."

Still, Europeans are reasonably guarded about the possible encroachment of U.S. regulation into Europe. Dr. Gerald Santing, director of the Netherlands Authority for the Financial Markets, explains how officials in Holland scrutinized the possibility that the New York Stock Exchange would impose U.S. rules on Euronext. "While it was decided that there was not too much a risk of spillover at the moment, the problem is still that you don't know what future legislation there might be."

Regardless of what might happen legislatively over time, crises could erupt at any moment. What is the role regulators play across borders when an emergency situation arises? The U.S. SEC and the CFTC might feel it necessary to apply every rule they can. The White House, conversely, might be opposed for political reasons.

Walter Lukken of the CFTC explains that it is a matter of balance. "We have to have enough independence to react to emergency crisis situations, and—we hope using our best judgment—do what's right for the marketplace. But if we step outside of that mission, Congress and the President should hold us accountable. So, there's this constant, healthy tension, and we're always trying to strike that balance. We stay in close contact with both during a crisis situation."

In the United States, the President's Working Group was formed following the 1987 U.S. stock market crash and plays a coordinating role during crises. The group comprises the secretary of the treasury, the chairman of the Federal Reserve Board, the SEC chairman, and the CFTC chairman. They meet frequently to discuss cross-jurisdictional issues and the lessons from past crises, which enables what Lukken describes as a constant information flow between the agencies and the White House. "We try to keep everybody informed and let them know what's going on," he says, "and hope that the tension between independence and accountability is the right balance."

SELF-REGULATION

In a world of demutualization, one of the key regulatory issues is that of *self-regulation* of what have become for-profit exchanges. "One impetus for the combination of New York Stock Exchange regulation and NASD regulation," explains Mary Schapiro, "was this tension between a for-profit publicly owned market, with its need to return value to shareholders, and the desire of the SEC and Congress that exchanges spend significantly on regulation and market surveillance. Separating off a significant piece of the regulatory burden to an independent self-regulating organization largely alleviates that tension for the New York Stock Exchange. It also helps take care of the lingering question of whether there are conflicts of interest in running a for-profit market and regulating that market's participants."

In Europe, much of what exchanges used to do themselves has moved to regulators, changing what had been a more informal, but still effective, compliance environment. The consensus seems to be that compliance in Europe has remained at an effective level despite the change. But no matter on which side of the Atlantic we look, we continue to see a mix of government regulation and self-regulation.

Mary Schapiro, the FINRA chief executive officer, describes how her organization helps create a balance. "For us, self-regulation is really about deep and broad industry participation in our process, but also about the ability for us to do things the government cannot do. We educate the industry, provide tools so industry can meet its compliance burdens and obligations, and work with industry to solve problems. Our board is 50 percent industry, and we are fully funded by the industry—about $600 million a year, which is not an insignificant tax on the business. But we do not own or operate exchanges. We do regulate some exchanges by a contract, but it's an arms-length contract and it's not an ownership interest that puts us in that relationship."

What about conflicts? Schapiro continues: "So, we have fewer conflicts, although I would never say we're conflict free. We can act with less legal formality as a self-regulating organization than can the SEC, and because we're as large as we are and we're spread out around the country, we're able to be closer to the industry. Yes, we bring enforcement cases, and yes, we write rules, but we are able to be as much a partner as a regulator. I think that is extremely difficult in the governmental context."

On the futures market side, the tensions are the same. "We took a different tack, to get more independence on the self-regulatory front," says Walter Lukken of the CFTC. "We looked at the for-profit structure of exchanges and felt that self-regulation has certain inherent conflicts. But it also has benefits: being closer to the marketplace, having expertise and understanding, being quicker to action than regulators often are. We understood that there needed to be more independence, and we really looked at the governance structure of exchanges and decided to create the independence within the structure itself."

The CFTC's approach, beginning in 2006, was to require public directors on all boards of exchanges. One-third of the exchange's board has to be nonmember, nonconflicted directors, and the exchange's regulatory oversight committee, which oversees all the regulatory functions, also must be made up of completely independent, public directors. "This establishes accountability," explains Lukken. "If something goes wrong on the regulatory side, the exchange has a nonconflicted director to report to and, ultimately, must also report to us. While we haven't gone quite as far as the securities side, we see the value in self-regulation."

These are but some of the changes and challenges facing the financial exchanges. Others relate to technology, which is changing at such a relentlessly fast pace that it's almost impossible to keep up. That topic is the focus of our next chapter.

Chapter 2

Technology Is Driving Change

Introduction

If demutualization represents the most fundamental structural change in the world of financial exchanges, the relentless pace of technology cannot be far behind. New information technologies have affected, and continue to alter, the process flow in financial exchanges, from market access through trading and all the way to the very important clearing and settlement process.

Technologies also, one might argue, change the very nature of what we mean by a financial exchange. Peter Bennett, solutions principal at HCL Technologies and a founder of Tradepoint, argues that "execution venues" is a more apt description due to the wide diversity—driven by technology—of exchange-like services and solutions. Consider the New York Stock Exchange as an "execution venue": There is a physical market floor *and* electronic trading, with market-making intervention by specialists.

Whatever the descriptive term one chooses, execution is key, and there is a lot more technological change on the horizon. This change is making trading activity better and less costly. In fact, price is perhaps the key determinant of whether a new technology succeeds in the exchange space. The price of a transaction is important, but so too is the price of executing a large block of shares in a short amount of time. It all comes back to the quality of the execution process. And, of course, the clearing and settlement costs are absolutely key as well.

"PLUMBING" INNOVATIONS

Let's look at some of the key technological innovations of the last few years and the prospects for more. The first is what Bennett calls part of the "plumbing." One example is the use of extranets—private networks that use network connectivity and Internet protocols to share information and operations among a business and its vendors, partners, customers, suppliers, and anyone else. Extranets make it possible to put the execution venue very close to a customer, as close as the customer's computer.

In a sense, as Bennett explains, "The plumbing could actually become the market itself and is well on the way to becoming the market." Others even imagine a future where the plumbing no longer exists and where all the major players—investment banks, hedge funds, and so on—have their computers in one room, shared by many execution venues. Beyond that is the concept of *virtualization*, where applications are simply loaded on a huge array of PC-like machines in a back room somewhere. Some software developers are even claiming that they have created the ability to move an order book around the world within a network of commodity servers.

PLUMBING

The word *plumbing* is used routinely in discussing the financial markets; it refers generally to the legal and regulatory framework, custody, clearing and settlement, and mechanisms for liquidity provision, taxes, and so on. In other words, plumbing is the *infrastructure*.

The analogy to the plumbing in a building is obvious. And like the plumbing in your home, financial plumbing is, as the European Commission sees it, "vital, but unglamorous and forgotten until something goes wrong."[1] In financial markets, plumbing needs to be in good working order.

Financial firms handle the plumbing in their markets in different ways. Some function more like regulated utilities, handling essential plumbing but bearing little risk. Others are risk seekers, aggressively looking for every angle to play and every opportunity to capture.

Then there's the bigger picture. As Charles R. Morris writes, "The financial sector is the economy's plumbing system. A company's failure, even a big one like IBM's, is like a broken sink, but a failure in the financial sector threatens the entire water supply."[2]

What all this speaks to is that the pace of technology is challenging the idea of an exchange in a fixed location. Execution venues can move to wherever the business needs to be.

David Lester is the chief information officer of the London Stock Exchange. He has seen a lot of technological change, which has occurred in what he describes as "three waves." The first came with what is known in London as "Big Bang," the 1986 deregulation of the market. Owner-ship of member firms by an outside corporation was allowed. All firms became broker/dealers able to operate in a dual capacity. Minimum scales of commission were abolished. Individual members ceased having

---

[1]European Commission, "Financial Markets Infrastructure," at http://ec.europa.eu/internal_market/financial-markets/index_en.htm; accessed March 22, 2008.
[2]Charles R. Morris, *Money, Greed, and Risk: Why Financial Crises and Crashes Happen*, New York: Times Business/Random House, 1999.

voting rights. And trading moved from being conducted face to face on a market floor to being performed via computer and telephone from separate dealing rooms.

"Big Bang in London put together a whole plethora of systems that supported the market at that stage," explains Lester. "It really closed the exchange floor and allowed traders to retreat back into the banks to watch a yellow strip and then basically ring each other up when they wanted to execute a trade. They could then report it into another system of the exchange."

That was the first wave. Next came the period between 1993 and 1997, when the London Stock Exchange introduced the public limit auto book. "We built a system called SETS, which was basically designed to replace the plethora of systems that had been put together in Big Bang," says Lester. SETS, for Stock Exchange Electronic Trading Service, aimed to bring greater speed and efficiency to the market. The initiative removed a lot of the existing information technology architectures and complexities.

The third wave is the one in which David Lester has primarily been involved—the Technology Roadmap. It began in March 2003, when Lester went to the exchange board and explained that SETS, while ultra-reliable, was too expensive and too hard to change. SETS was built in COBOL, and, as Lester explains, "It would take us nine months to make simple kinds of functional changes to the system. It would take us nine months to do a capacity upgrade and costs us 10 million quid."

The Technology Roadmap, when first outlined, aimed "to achieve about £8m in technology cost savings, while boosting scalability and enabling the company to add new markets quickly and easily."[3] It was motivated also by the need to realize consistency of performance when the market needs it most.

The final piece of the Technology Roadmap is Tradelect, the London Stock Exchange's electronic trading system that went live in June 2007. It makes it possible for trades to be executed fully and resiliently in about 10 milliseconds. It also increases the exchange's capacity by a

---

[3]James Watson, "LSE aims for cost cuts with systems update," *Computing*, February 23, 2005, at www.accountancyagejobs.com/computing/news/2071538/lse-aims-cost-cuts-systems-update; accessed March 3, 2008.

factor of five. "Tradelect removes all of the limitations of SETS and really sets the London market free," contends Lester.

Lester's innovation is on a massive scale. Other plumbing technologies are being developed by smaller firms that are using tools aimed at making it possible to introduce software products and services within days of their conception, without having to involve expensive programmers and leaving the important decisions in their hands.

Beyond the old-line, established exchanges, we are seeing a growing number of new technology-driven exchanges that exist primarily as online markets. For instance, PLUS Markets plc has established what it describes as a "fully competitive equity stock exchange in London, offering a deep pool of liquidity across over 7,500 U.K. and European securities."[4]

Technological innovations make markets such as PLUS possible. Market makers provide quotes on the market. They have their own negotiation network and they trade reporting into the market. Pricing and the price discovery process are determined with the use of a reference market, which could even be the London Stock Exchange.

As Brian Taylor, the PLUS Markets chief financial officer and head of information technology, explains, "This is the combination of highly scalable technology implemented in an innovative way with some business rules that promote liquidity and without the costs of the clearing and settlement infrastructure."

INNOVATIONS ON THE BACK END

The back-end clearing and settlement processes are undergoing technological change elsewhere, too. The DTCC and NYMEX clearing, as well as other clearinghouses in New York and Chicago, are wrestling with new services and new technologies. NYMEX has its ClearPort,[5] where trades executed bilaterally as over-the-counter derivative trades, for example, can be novated to NYMEX clearing, converted into ladders of futures contracts, and cleared and settled through futures

[4]www.plusmarketsgroup.com/; accessed March 3, 2008.
[5]www.nymex.com/cp_overview.aspx; accessed June 6, 2008.

commissions merchants in the same way as regular NYMEX transactions. The effect of using this technology has been to eliminate major levels of credit risk from the OTC derivatives market.

Getting ClearPort up and going was quite a process for NYMEX. It began with what was almost a manual process by which trades were both novated up to the clearinghouse and set up there, but automation, enabled by new technology, has made it possible for the process to compete on the basis of its straight-through processing (STP)[6] qualities.

With respect to post-transaction processing, the DTCC's Deriv/SERV is a very good example. Seeing an opportunity, DTCC set up an automated matching and confirmation service for OTC derivatives trades, including credit, equity, and interest rate derivatives. Deriv/SERV also provides related matching of payment flows and bilateral netting services. The technology has resulted in fundamental changes in how OTC derivatives, particularly credit derivatives, are confirmed in the United States. Further, Deriv/SERV is an example of the way technology can expand a customer base. For DTCC, it has opened up an entirely new class of customers. Beyond the broker-dealers, the customer base also includes hedge funds and any other party that trades credit derivatives.

DTCC's process innovation with technology extends to one of the most leading-edge changes in the clearing and settlement process. In December 2006, DTCC launched a Trade Information Warehouse to reduce the manual component in post-trade processing of OTC derivatives transactions. The warehouse has two components: a comprehensive trade database that holds the "official legal record" for all contracts eligible for automated Deriv/SERV confirmation, and a central support infrastructure to automate and standardize post-trade processes over each contract's lifetime, including payments, notional adjustments, and contract term changes.[7]

Here is an example of technology driving a major market structure change and taking a major cost out of the system. And it has implications

---

[6]www.mondovisione.com/index.cfm?section=articles&action=detail&id=68956; accessed June 6, 2008.
[7]"DTCC Launches OTC Derivatives Trade Information Warehouse," *The Trade News*, December 13, 2006, at www.thetradenews.com/trading/otc-derivatives/105; accessed March 13, 2008.

for equity derivatives and interest rate derivatives as well as credit derivatives. That is DTCC's plan. "Initially, the warehouse will support credit derivatives and then extend to other OTC derivatives products including rates, equities, FX, and commodities—depending on market demand and input from the senior group working with DTCC in guiding the initiative."[8] Even energy transactions could be put into the warehouse. At DTCC, technology is solving some of the fundamental problems in the OTC derivatives sector that have existed for decades.

INNOVATIONS IN TRADE EXECUTION

At the trade execution level, technology is facilitating some significant improvements in price, speed, and the products that can be offered to investors and other players. Electronic communication networks (ECNs) have increasingly eliminated the need for third parties in the execution of orders entered by market makers on exchanges or over the counter. At the same time, new market makers unknown to most only a few short years ago are emerging as dominant players in the business, at least in the United States.

Instinet Group LLC, founded in 1969, is the oldest and largest of the ECNs. The firm uses its Internet-based electronic platform to match stock buyers and sellers and process transactions instantaneously. Instinet members, primarily professional traders and investors, can display bid and offer quotes for stocks and transact between themselves using brokers.

The firm's technology "eliminated the need for a team of in-house brokers [and] allowed it to charge lower transaction fees and stay open 24 hours a day, seven days a week. Even more important, however, was Instinet's ability to offer anonymity. Because traditional traders would quite often have to deal with several other brokers before closing a deal, the potential for information leaks was high; as a result, using Instinet as a trading vehicle was seen by many large companies, particularly other traders like mutual fund companies, as a way to avoid unwanted publicity—quite often a cause of major market fluctuations—regarding

---

[8] *Ibid.*

the purchase and sale of large chunks of stock."[9] Instinet and other ECNs have, over the years, evolved into major threats to the established stock exchanges—thanks to technology.

THE RISE OF ECNs

Instinet began in 1969 and was the first ECN in the financial markets. But it wasn't until nearly 30 years later that ECNs really made their mark. *Business Week* put it this way:

> *Once upon a time, the New York Stock Exchange traded big-company stocks on a central trading floor at its marble-colonnaded building overlooking Wall Street. Its rival, the NASDAQ stock market, traded small-company shares through an electronic dealer network. Until a few years ago, the two exchanges were happy within their distinct market structures, each of which thrived because they satisfied the capital-raising needs of different corporations.*[10]

But the ECNs attracted the "high-tech behemoths like Microsoft, Intel, and Dell" —and NYSE couldn't lure them away. The "Big Board" was, to use *Business Week*'s term, "spooked."

It wasn't supposed to work out that way. And even in light of NYSE's apparent efforts to transform itself into an electronic trading platform, motivated by the competitive threat of the ECNs, many analysts were still predicting the demise of electronic trading not many months later.

Writing in an "Electronic Trading" supplement to *Risk* magazine in November 1999, Deborah Williams described ECNs as a "short-lived phenomenon." Her prediction went like this: "The popularity of ECNs means that they could even form an evolutionary prelude to something

---

[9]Free Encyclopedia of eCommerce, at http://ecommerce.hostip.info/pages/591/Instinet-Group-LLC.html; accessed March 7, 2008.
[10]Paula Dwyer and Mike McNamee, "Why the Bourses Are Spooked," *Business Week* Online, March 15, 1999, at www.businessweek.com/1999/99_11/b3620091.htm; accessed March 22, 2008.

larger and permanent—the creation of an electronic, order-driven stock market. But if this happens, ECNs threaten to become a victim of their own success, as the need for ECNs would soon disappear, and their fall could be just as quick as their ascent."[11]

Williams was correct in one respect: Some ECNs would disappear. But it was not the fault of the ECN business model; rather, the exigencies of competition and other factors in the business environment shook out the playing field. Not many years after her analysis, we could read this in *Waters* magazine: " A new generation of ECNs has popped up, while old ones are getting a fresh coat of paint."[12]

The article notes, "After the New York Stock Exchange (NYSE) acquired the Archipelago Exchange and Nasdaq Stock Market acquired the Inet trading venue from Instinet in the first quarter of last year, Wall Street all but wrote the obituaries for the remaining electronic communication networks (ECNs). However, the industry forgot to mention this to the last surviving ECNs."

Today we find the ECNs to be a formidable group of players in the world's financial markets—whether they go it alone, as partners of the old exchanges, or in joint ventures with the new venues coming online.

In a nutshell, technology has been driving dramatic changes in traditional market making, particularly in the past few years. Is specialist market making the next frontier for automation? Specialist markets are automated to a degree. Traditional market makers, thanks to their own electronic communications networks, are putting considerable pressure on the specialists. The bottom line is that with all the technology driving the trading world, it is simply no longer feasible to remain on the floor.

[11]Deborah Williams, "A short-lived phenomenon," *Risk* Electronic Trading Supplement, November 1999, at www.financewise.com/public/edit/riskm/e-trading/etrading-ecns.htm; accessed March 22, 2008.
[12]Rob Daly, "The Fall and Rise of ECNs," *Waters*, March 1, 2006, at www.watersonline.com/public/showPage.html?page=318474; accessed March 22, 2008.

The degree of importance given to technological prowess is illustrated by the example of BATS, founded in June 2005 "to make markets better through technology, process, and price innovation."[13] This was a time when "market innovation and technology leadership were at risk due to over consolidation in the ECN and exchange industry. Independent market centers were being bought up, and the number of credible places to trade were rapidly decreasing." What makes BATS successful, some argue, is not that it is faster or less expensive than other cutting-edge, technology-driven competitors but that it has product. That product is liquidity. After only 18 months, BATS enjoyed a 10 percent share of the market for all NASDAQ trades.

The BATS world headquarters is in Kansas City, and not even in the downtown financial district. It could be anywhere, however, including in someone's garage. Technology makes it possible for people with a good idea to employ the available advanced network connectivity and have a real impact.

Project Turquoise

On a much larger scale, there is the technology behind Project Turquoise, an equities trading platform being designed by nine major investment banks: BNP Paribas, Citigroup, Credit Suisse, Deutsche Bank, Goldman Sachs, Merrill Lynch, Morgan Stanley, Société Générale, and UBS. The objective is a system—a pan-European platform based in London—that provides dealing services at less than half the price of traditional exchanges; it is at the same time a hybrid allowing trading both on and off traditional exchanges. Why are the banks so serious about creating an alternative now? Some explain it as a combination of the regulatory environment, technological advances, and the natural cycle of ownership in industries. At this writing, after some delays, it is scheduled for a September 2008 launch.[14]

[13]"About Us," BATS, at www.batstrading.com/about_us.php; accessed March 13, 2008.

[14]Luke Jeffs, "Turquoise exec is counting down to September launch," *Financial News Online US*, at www.financialnews-us.com/?page=ushome&contentid=2450144651; accessed March 26, 2008.

WHO'S BEHIND TURQUOISE?

With one exception, the nine investment banks that launched Project Turquoise are all among the "Bloomberg 20"—the world's 20 largest, according to *Bloomberg Markets*, as measured by total fees.[15] The breadth and scope of their reach is remarkable.

Citigroup[16] sits in the top slot, with $6.88 billion in fees in 2007. Better known as Citi, it was formed from the merger of Citicorp and Travelers Group in April 1988. The Forbes Global 2000, an annual ranking since 2003 of the top 2,000 public companies in the world, ranks New York–based Citi as the 24th-largest company worldwide, with total assets just shy of $2.2 trillion as of December 2007.[17] Citi holds more than 200 million customer accounts in more than 100 countries.

Next on the Bloomberg 20 list comes Goldman Sachs,[18] in a close second slot with $6.66 in fees in 2007. Goldman Sachs was founded in 1869 and became a member of the New York Stock Exchange in 1896. The New York–headquartered bank's rich history includes having been one of the firms that established a market for initial public offerings in the early 20th century. Goldman Sachs sits just above Citi in the Forbes Global 2000, at number 23 worldwide. Total assets as of December 2007 were about $1.2 trillion.

In third place on the Bloomberg 20 we find Morgan Stanley,[19] with $6.36 billion in fees in 2007. The bank began in 1935, in the midst of the Great Depression. At number 75 on the Forbes Global 2000 list, Morgan Stanley, also based in New York City, had just over $1 trillion in total assets as of December 2007.

Continued

[15] The full list for 2007 can be viewed at www.bloomberg.com/news/marketsmag/mm_0408_story1.html; accessed April 5, 2008.
[16] www.citigroup.com/citigroup/homepage/, accessed April 5, 2008.
[17] "The Global 2000," *Forbes*, at www.forbes.com/lists/2008/18/biz_2000global08_The-Global-2000_Rank.html; accessed April 9, 2008. The Forbes list is compiled based on four metrics: sales, profits, assets, and market value.
[18] www2.goldmansachs.com, accessed April 5, 2008.
[19] www.morganstanley.com/, accessed April 5, 2008.

WHO'S BEHIND TURQUOISE?—Continued

Merrill Lynch,[20] which sits in the fifth spot on the Bloomberg 20 with $5.55 billion in fees in 2007, also goes back a long way. Founded in 1915, the company is way down the Forbes Global 2000 list compared with the other Turquoise founders, at number 431. Total assets in December 2007 were just over $1 trillion, but negative profits tell the story of New York-based Merrill Lynch's rank.

Like Merrill Lynch, UBS[21]—although ranked sixth on the Bloomberg 20 with $4.58 billion in fees in 2007—suffers in the Forbes Global 2000 rankings because of negative profits. In 386th place, the Swiss-based bank had assets of just over $2 trillion in December 2007. UBS is the largest bank in Switzerland and traces its roots back to a bank established in 1747.

Credit Suisse[22] sits in seventh place on the Bloomberg 20, with $4.58 billion in fees in 2007. It is the second-largest Swiss bank, behind UBS. Ranked 43rd on the Forbes Global 2000, UBS had total assets of nearly $1.2 trillion in December 2007. It was founded in 1856.

At number eight on the Bloomberg 20 list, Deutsche Bank[23] had fees in 2007 totaling $4.41 billion. The bank began its life in 1870 in Berlin, specializing in foreign trade. Today it is headquartered in Frankfurt, Germany. Deutsche Bank's Forbes Global 2000 ranking is number 32, with $1.5 trillion in assets in December 2007.

BNP Paribas, 15th on the Bloomberg 20 with $1.10 billion in fees in 2007, is based in Paris. One of Europe's main banks and one of France's "old three" (along with Sociéte Générale and Crédit Lyonnais), BNP was formed in May 2000 through the merger of Banque Nationale de Paris, founded in 1869, and Paribas. Today the bank sits at number 13 on the Forbes Global 2000, with total assets of $2.5 trillion in December 2007. Among banks alone (i.e., without other industries added to the mix), BNP Paribas ranks highest, in fifth place.

---

[20]www.ml.com, accessed April 5, 2008.
[21]www.ubs.com/, accessed April 5, 2008.
[22]www.credit-suisse.com/us/en/, accessed April 5, 2008.
[23]www.db.com/index_e.htm, accessed April 5, 2008.

The remaining Turquoise founder is Société Générale,[24] which fell off the most recent Bloomberg 20 list. The bank, headquartered in Paris, was founded in 1864. The Forbes Global 2000 puts it in 102nd place, with total assets of nearly $1.6 trillion in December 2007.

It is notable that for all the attention to Project Turquoise, these banks rarely discuss their controversial initiative, at least on their Websites. A search of the corporate Websites of all nine investment banks produces not a single mention of Project Turquoise by any of the U.S.-based banks. Deutsche Bank "hits" can be found only on the bank's national Websites for Belgium and Hungary; there are none on the corporate site. UBS provides a couple of documents about Turquoise appointing EuroCCP for clearing and settlement, and that is all. On the BNP Paribas corporate Website, a search on *turquoise* results in a lot of information about the bank's sponsorship an international tennis match and the fact that about a third of women players, in a vote, chose the color turquoise for courtside banners.

CONTROVERSY

Project Turquoise is not without controversy, not the least of which has been a nagging belief among some that the purpose at first was not to build a real exchange but to bluff the London Stock Exchange and others into reducing trading prices. Today, though, Turquoise touts itself as "a much-needed alternative to the incumbent exchanges."[25] Its founding members invested to "give traders freedom to choose among liquidity venues."

Robert Barnes, managing director of equities at UBS Investment Bank, explains that UBS has two messages: "We wish to work in a spirit of entrepreneurial partnership with Exchanges to promote liquidity and new business, and there are two ways we can work together: commercially and structurally. Commercially, these include simpler tariffs that incentivize incremental flow, and structurally this means promotion of best practice key criteria shared by successful markets such as anonymity of broker identifiers for a more level playing field,

[24]www.sgcib.com/, accessed April 5, 2008.
[25]www.tradeturquoise.com/, accessed March 26, 2008.

good rules for crossing, direct execution, derivatives and meaningful securities borrowing and lending." The second UBS message is to say, "Thank you to the Regulators for establishing a framework that encourages the free market alternative of competitive new entry." Barnes adds that Turquoise—as a new platform—is expected to offer "competitive new entry for order books and some form of smart anonymous block trading" complementing visible continuous trading with functionality for dark liquidity.

Philip Hylander, the global head of equities trading for Goldman Sachs (one of the Project Turquoise partners), thinks there is a lot of room for improvement where the investment banks have something to offer—clearing, for instance. "Anybody who really digs into clearing and looks at the pricing structure and the margins understands that it doesn't take a neurosurgeon to take a scalpel to the costs," says Hylander. "These are businesses that have operated largely immune from competition—and it goes without saying that they would therefore enjoy enormous operating margins." Noting Citigroup's entry into the clearing and settlement business, Hylander sees it as a plus. "The introduction of Citi into this is workable, first and foremost, very scalable because of Citi's size, and actually very cost effective."

In relation to Turquoise, Hylander sees Citi's clearing business as another example of cost savings. "Representatives of Turquoise have gone on record as saying they expect to deliver savings on post-trade of at least 50 percent. It may be easy for some other people to presuppose that this is just going to be incredibly expensive and won't do anything, but if flow migrates to this marketplace it will provide cheap trading and clearing and settlement. And it is designed to do so." The clearing business is no different.

Still, many concerns about Turquoise linger. Chris Hohn of The Children's Investment Fund promotes exchanges because of nervousness over being able to route his order flow through the machinery of something like Turquoise and knowing that it will be secure and safe. He expresses concern about getting the best execution and not being picked off by aggressive market makers somewhere within the investment bank organizations. Others worry about Turquoise's intention to integrate dark and transparent pools of liquidity. In a dark pool, the order book is hidden from participants, and they do not know the bid/ask price in the pool. This makes it possible for traders to park huge blocks of shares in the order book without signaling market participants.

Some believe that the big investment banks that founded Turquoise will use this feature to exercise market power.

Barnes explains that Turquoise will have to survive on its own merits, commercially and functionally. And as far as a rule book, he says, "When the rules are clarified, they will be made transparent to the public, just like with the London Stock Exchange. Then it will be up to us as sell-side brokers, as we choose the venues, to make sure we can deliver the best execution, the best possible result, for our clients based on the merits at the time."

One question that has been raised about Turquoise is how it should be characterized. Is it a mutual or demutualized organization? Philip Hylander says, "You can think of it as the remutualization of the market. It is an organization formed by a group of investment banks, but once the management team is in place,[26] these banks will merely be shareholders. They will not be the sole members of the exchange. It will just be an alternative trading venue."

If Hylander's characterization is accurate, it stands to reason that with other members beyond the founding banks coming on board the new exchange would be open, down the road, to other shareholders. That suggests listing Turquoise for trading on an exchange. Some question the argument, then, that Turquoise is a response to "high" payments by the founding banks for their participation in the London Stock Exchange, Euronext, and so on. And might this not mean a continuous cycle of demutualization, remutualization, and again demutualization—*ad infinitum*?

THE CYCLE OF COMPETITION

Hylander sees it as a reflection of the cycles through which every industry goes. "Every industry has cycles of consolidation and then cycles of increased growth," he notes. It is a natural part of industries that operate in a competitive environment. In a sense, it is the cost of there being competition."

What is the alternative, from Hylander's perspective? "There is another option," he notes. "We could have a heavily regulated industry

---

[26]Which, since Hylander spoke, has occurred.

with price controls. The problem with that, of course, is that while price regulation deals with prices—which is a good thing—it doesn't really deal with innovation. And we need innovation as well."

To Hylander and many others, it is a simple question. "Are you prepared to tolerate a little bit of this cycle of competition, and then fragmentation, and then reconsolidation in order to get the benefits both in price and in quality of service?" asks Hylander. "We vote yes, because we think that technology has evolved to a point where that cycle is pretty rapid."

Tony Mackay, president and managing director of Instinet Europe, sees Turquoise as a technological advance. "At Instinet, we've got a trading platform that out of the box can handle every market in the world. Turquoise will be able to start straight out of the box, too, offering a pan-European solution. And that's actually very interesting when you add the clearing solution as well. It's one of the big costs of trading in Europe. You might be long stocks in France, short stocks in Germany, and at the end of the day you have to maintain different margins in those two countries. There's no pan-European way to offset the fact that trading really is pan-European. The benefit of a pan-European central counter party that is able to then plug the delivery of the shares into the central depositories—that is a new mousetrap that is a better mousetrap."

Mackay sees Turquoise as a catalyst to help solve the problem of pan-European clearing. Why is it so important? He provides a hypothetical situation. "If a clearinghouse goes bust," explains Mackay, "normal bankruptcy laws would dictate that everything is then frozen. A liquidator could come in and say he'll keep the cash or keep the stock, liquidate those, but not give any cash to people. You have to have special legislation so the clearinghouses can actually settle the trades going through. On a pan-European basis, that's not in place yet. We're having to write the rules as we go along, and I think the benefit of having Turquoise and Chi-X[27] is that it's going to be easier for the second person to do it, and then easier for the third person. The regulatory environment in Europe is going to make this possible. And, in probably two or three years, we will end up with a set of rules and regulations that cover pre-, during, and post-trading that we can all operate with. We're not there yet, but it's a work in progress."

---

[27]Chi-X is an Instinet trading platform.

Lehman Brothers is one of the major investment banks that did not help found Turquoise. Xavier Rolet, the managing director for Lehman Brothers Europe, explains that his firm takes a neutral stance on Turquoise. "As a firm, we are pro-competition in the exchange field, or in your clearing field, and in the whole exchange infrastructure environment," says Rolet. "For us, it is a question of how impatient you want to be about the way things are today. Clearly, there are innovative forms of trading and some that are actually not that innovative that have been around for a while. We definitely want to continue to support them. And there's no doubt that certain kinds of trading are hampered by excessive exchange charges, especially in the fast-growing segments of the market."

For Rolet, Turquoise poses some fundamental questions about financial markets in general and how they should operate. "At the end of the day, you have here in the capital markets a convergence of many interests—retail versus wholesale investment banks, corporate issuers, the general public, all sorts of constituencies or stakeholders. Whether it is owned privately or publicly, regardless of its capital structure, an exchange—if it works properly—is a neutral venue where all participants, all users, can have their interests represented."

THE RULEBOOK

What, then, might the issue with Turquoise be, from this perspective? Rolet explains, "We believe that one of the major ways that neutrality is represented is the rulebook. And how is the rulebook determined? We have to ask ourselves—and this is not to denigrate the Turquoise initiative—how do you look at a new exchange venue that is, in effect, structured by one of its user constituencies? How is that rulebook going to reflect the interest of the users at large? How is technology going to be set up? How might the ownership structure potentially influence decisions, such as those around clearing?"

Lehman Brothers has taken what Rolet characterizes as a "fairly cautious attitude" with respect to Turquoise, and chose not to participate in the beginning. Rolet believes that more questions should be asked. "How does it serve the investing public at large for banks to get into the exchange business, then out of the exchange business, and then back into the exchange business? Outside of our own proprietary flow, which obviously belongs to us, the rest of the business we do on exchanges or out of exchanges is entrusted to us by clients. We want to be very careful to direct that flow in a fashion that does not look potentially conflicted. And whatever we may say or do, at the end of the day, the choice is not going to be with us, it's going to be with our clients."

The founders of Turquoise continue to provide assurances and calming words, and the project marches forward. Yet some skepticism prevails. David Lester of the London Stock Exchange puts it this way: "There is a role exchanges play where they think about the entire market and look after the interests of the whole. If I were to say that I believe Turquoise was all about exchange fees, it would be something I don't genuinely believe. Still, I would welcome any initiative, and I think the market will decide. If there's a value proposition there, Turquoise will succeed, and I think the pie will increase."

New entrants, whether small or large like Turquoise, should in theory offer price improvements and better trading opportunities. Otherwise, there is little point in their existence. Technology plays a key role because, from a value proposition perspective, new entrants must figure out what kinds of price improvements they can offer, which means that they must innovate with products and services.

"When competition came to the U.S. market," says Instinet's Tony Mackay, "Instinet was essentially the only electronic marketplace. We had the electronic monopoly. Within three years, we had to cut our prices by 95 percent. Shares in Instinet went from $20 to $3. Reuters, our parent, went from £15 to under £1. Over a three-year period, we had to rewrite our matching engine three times just to compete. And we actually had to merge with Island, which had been the new kid on the block that had actually eaten a lot of our lunch. There's no reason not to believe this isn't going to happen in Europe—but competition is actually good. Competition is the thing that is going to drive this."

Turquoise, believes Mackay, is nothing to fear, and new technology makes it that much more desirable to have it as part of the competitive landscape. "Within Chi-X, we're building essentially a commodity-smart router. If an order comes to Chi-X and there's a better price on the exchanges or on Turquoise or anywhere else that starts up, we will automatically route to those venues. People should have the confidence to go to these new venues. We can build a smart router, and that will do certain things, but so can the investment banks themselves. It all adds value to their clients. So far, the exchanges haven't shown the willingness to pass order flow onto Chi-X or Turquoise, if there's a better price. But I know Chi-X will, and I'm sure Turquoise will, offer that on routing. Once that happens, you really do break down the barriers for people trying the new venues. You point your order to Chi-X or Turquoise or whoever you decide you want to go to first, and then they actually take care of your best execution obligations."

Regardless of any individual opinion or speculation about Turquoise, though, the consensus is that technology is fueling new innovations all the time. Let's look at one class of technological advance on the buy side—direct market access—and the impact it is having on the future of the financial markets.

Direct Market Access

To understand the importance of *direct market access* (DMA) technology, we first need to consider what the buy side itself says about what it does, the role it plays, the way it accesses markets, and so on. By way of introduction, what does an exchange provide to the buy side?

A few things are critical. First are the best price and the best liquidity. As Giovanni Beliossi, managing partner at FGS Capital LLP in London, sees it, "Liquidity is important, certainly, but it is more important to get the price that we want."

Transparency is also critical. Without transparency, it is impossible to know whether the price is, indeed, the best. Transparency is also the means by which the buy side knows that a trade is free of conflicts of interest.

Growing DMA is changing the way the buy side does business. DMA refers to electronic facilities that allow buy-side firms to more directly access liquidity for financial securities they might want to buy or sell. It allows institutional traders to aggregate liquidity that is fragmented. It gives buy-side firms greater control over their trading strategies. As one writer has put it, "With DMA, they are renting a broker's infrastructure and clearing via the broker, but they are controlling the order."[28] Plus aggressive DMA trading saves a lot of money on commissions.

---

[28]Ivy Schmerken, "Direct-Market-Access Trading," *Wall Street & Technology*, February 4, 2005, at www.wallstreetandtech.com/features/showArticle.jhtml? articleID=59301336; accessed February 9, 2008.

BANKS AND DMA

Banks in their role as buy-side traders are especially fond of DMA, though perhaps they don't need the tool. Chris Hohn, the founder and managing director of The Children's Investment Fund, believes that when it comes to investment banks and DMA, the exchanges have a crucial role to play.

"Banks today make more money from proprietary trading than commissions as an agent," says Hohn, "so they are heavily incented to try to see and take advantage of the flow of buy side participants. Even in the case of direct market access, banks have the ability to see that flow, and the bank's head of trading can walk into the room where DMA is taking place, and there's really actually no need at all to have direct market access through an investment bank."

Hohn continues, "I think this is a real critical point that is never really talked about. In a world where banks see flow and are able to use that information to trade against the user, you cannot have immense value. It's a reason that investment banks make billions of dollars of profits from trading. They see flow and that ends up working against the client. That is a very important reason that exchanges play such a critical role."

Given the way banks use DMA tools, does it make a difference whether others on the buy side use DMA tools sponsored by an agency broker or someone with a proprietary trading desk? Hohn believes that, ideally, the tool would be owned by someone independent, with no proprietary trading. Beliossi largely agrees and adds, "We are going from a situation in which most traditional buy side players who are still major contributors to trading have been going from a very intermediated and very costly way of trading through investment banks, to a situation in which more and more of that trading is executed without intermediaries. This is true despite the hedge funds. These trades are getting much closer to an execution that is direct, either through an exchange or simply peer to peer."

With this tension between investment banks and others on the buy side, the question of whether exchanges might provide more neutrality than a system such as, say, Project Turquoise, is an obvious one. Our look at the future of the financial markets, it seems, circles back to Project Turquoise with some frequency. However, keeping with the technology theme, let's look at the derivatives markets. They provide a very good illustration of technology, playing its role with other advances, helping to drive growth. As we will see, technology is important—but it isn't everything.

Derivatives Markets

One of the most striking changes in the financial markets over the past few years has been the startling growth in derivatives trading.

Traditionally there have been two main markets: exchange-trade derivatives and over-the-counter derivatives. Exchange trading has tended to focus on standardized derivative contracts in a range of underlying products, whether they are options or futures. The OTC market focused on tailor-made derivatives, with investment banks serving as market makers and clients being drawn from commercial banks, pension funds, hedge funds, and other institutional investors. OTC trading usually involved swaps, forward contracts, forward rate agreements, credit derivatives, and similar products.

DERIVATIVES IN THE OTC SPACE

Today, exchange-traded derivatives are picking up their percentage of total derivatives volume traded, and derivatives exchanges are now moving into the traditional OTC space. Just how significant are the figures? Consider some statistics from NYSE Euronext for February 2008: "NYSE Euronext's derivatives trading operations recorded substantial gains in overall activity during February, with a 49% increase in total volume on Liffe and an 81% gain in total contracts traded on NYSE Arca Options year-to-date, compared to the same period in 2007. In February, Liffe traded almost 92 million futures and options contracts, representing an average daily volume of 4.4 million, up 31% from the same month in 2007. Bclear, Liffe's wholesale service for OTC trades, processed over 13 million contracts in February 2008, up 222% compared to the same month in 2007."[29]

---

[29]"NYSE Euronext Business Summary for February 2008," Press Release, March 4, 2008, at http://www.nyse.com/press/1204628974300.html; accessed March 7, 2008.

Liffe operates regulated, high-tech markets in Amsterdam, Brussels, Lisbon, and Paris, "where every day approximately two trillion euros worth of derivatives business is traded by customers from around the world."[30] It is NYSE Euronext's leading international derivatives business. NYSE Arca Options is NYSE Euronext's options trading platform.[31] The numbers NYSE Euronext reports for both Liffe and Arca are substantial indicators of a shift.

What is driving this shift? One element is that exchanges are doing a better job than ever of educating their customers about how to use the market. Exchanges are becoming competitive against the banks that had long held sway in the OTC space. Also, there is a growing need to manage risk. There is every reason to expect the migration of the OTC business to the exchanges so long as they can give customers the opportunity to stop carrying that risk on their books and shift it to the exchange clearinghouse.

Changing Client Base

Jim Newsome, president and chief executive officer of NYMEX, the New York Mercantile Exchange, sees the changing nature of the client base as one of the drivers of growth. "While our client base has probably changed less than some of the other exchanges—70 percent of our volume is still driven by our commercial entities—we are seeing more hedge funds and more of the financial sector moving the trading," says Newsome. "But from a percentage standpoint, that has been offset by increases in volume of commercial customers at this point."

David Krell, president and chief executive officer of the International Securities Exchange (ISE), observes that there has been a great deal of innovation and creativity on the part of exchanges and that new products as well as awareness and education have improved tremendously. These are fueling growth that promises to grow by even greater leaps and bounds.

---

[30]"Liffe Overview: Liffe Futures & Options," at www.euronext.com/landing/liffeLanding-12601-EN.html; accessed March 7, 2008.

[31]See www.nyse.com/productservices/nysearcaoptions/1151534050804.html.

Several things are helping shift the balance in options trading toward exchanges and away from the OTC market, Krell notes. "One, I think the market is much more efficient. The bid-ask spreads are much tighter than ever before. The displayed liquidity is much, much greater. All the exchanges now provide automated access. Efficiency is so much greater. Costs have been reduced, including the implicit cost of trading options."

Competition is also a factor, and it could well be that the options business is inherently more competitive than the financial futures business. Krell's business relies heavily on having market makers, lest liquidity would disperse across too many maturities and strike prices. That suggests that a better trading system alone will not attract people. The exchange must maintain good relations with those market makers.

"Market makers want to trade with customers," explains Krell, "so our main focus is to bring the customer into the exchange. If we're successful in doing so, the market makers will be there. We decided to create incentives both for the order flow to come in as well as for the liquidity providers to meet that order flow—and we did that by creating a more reliable, scalable system. We've also created incentives to people to provide a quote. Every time a market maker makes a market, they're giving someone a free option. The whole world is receiving that free option in terms of the bid and ask that they're providing out there. We have to give that entity, that firm, a *reason* to provide that free option to the world."

What ISE is doing appears to be working. Speaking from the equity options perspective, Krell notes, "I don't think many people realize that this business was dominated for decades by retail. Just seven years ago, probably 80 percent of the daily turnover in the industry was coming from individual investors. The efficiencies of the market have brought in a lot more institutional players than ever before. As you well recognize, professionals don't trade in inefficient markets, and that's basically what this market was in general just seven or 10 years ago. We estimate that today the institutional segment has grown to about 50 percent. I think we're in the infancy of growth in that segment, and that's why we've seen this secular shift and tremendous growth in volumes."

To buttress his assessment of the future, Krell points out that the main participants so far on the institutional side, at least in the options business, are the hedge funds. "We still have not made a great deal of penetration into the traditional asset management side," he points out. "In that regard, I think we're probably just in a second inning of growth. So we're very optimistic about the future."

In terms of the participants and what they look to do, there are some key differences between options and futures trading. Those differences, though, have become less apparent. Instruments are becoming more interchangeable as large institutions such as hedge funds employ a genuine portfolio strategy in everything they do.

PORTFOLIO MARGINING

Among the significant alterations in the market landscape over the past several years, portfolio margining is one of the most widely welcomed. Though it had been around on the commodities futures side of things for quite some time, it was not until the last couple of years that portfolio margining became available as a strategy in the derivatives markets. Essentially, it allows for one to look at the margin as a portfolio in an account, rather than the "old" way of looking at each component differently and separately.

PORTFOLIO MARGINING

The Securities and Exchange Commission defines portfolio margining as "a margin methodology that sets margin requirements for an account based on the greatest projected net loss of all positions in a product class or group as determined by the Commission-approved options pricing model using multiple pricing scenarios. These scenarios are designed to measure the theoretical loss of the positions given changes in both the underlying price and implied volatility inputs to the model. Accordingly, the margin required is based on the greatest loss that would be incurred in a portfolio if the value of its components move up or down by a predetermined amount."[32]

[32]U.S. Securities and Exchange Commission, "NYSE Rulemaking: Customer Portfolio and Cross-Margining Requirements," at www.sec.gov/rules/sro/34-46576.htm; accessed March 7, 2008.

In July 2005, the SEC approved a portfolio-margining pilot program, limited to broad-based index options and related exchange-traded funds and requiring that participating customers establish and maintain account equity of at least $5 million. In April 2007, new rules went into effect after the SEC eliminated the equity minimum and expanded the scope of products to include equities, equity options, narrow-based index options, and certain security futures products (including single-stock futures, described later in this chapter). The approved changes also eliminated the $5 million minimum account equity requirement.

Here is an example of how it works. Say you owned 1,000 shares of a $50 stock and you owned 10 puts on that stock at a 45 strike price. With the old margin calculations in the United States, you would have to put up 50 percent margin on the stock and then pay for the put in full. The "system," so to speak, did not recognize that put as the head for that stock. With portfolio margining allowed, though, the two are recognized as a combined entity: Your real risk in this position of holding a $50 stock and being on a 45 strike put is that difference of five points plus the cost of the put.

How was the SEC's action greeted by the options industry? The Options Clearing Corporation (described in detail later in this chapter) was certainly enthusiastic. "This expansion of customer portfolio margining helps U.S. equities markets take a major leap forward by allowing securities firms to participate on a level playing field with the futures and international equities markets with respect to customer margining."[33]

The importance of this SEC move to the future of the derivatives markets is significant. Randy Frederick, director of derivatives at Charles Schwab, echoed the sentiment of many brokers when he called it "one of the biggest fundamental changes to occur in [the] brokerage business in years."[34]

---

[33]The Options Clearing Corporation, "Customer Portfolio Margin (CPM)," at www.optionsclearing.com/products/cpm/default.jsp; accessed March 7, 2008.
[34]Quoted in Steven Smith, "The Brave New World of Portfolio Margining," RealMoney.com, April 5, 2007, at www.thestreet.com/pom/pomrmy/10348598.html; accessed March 7, 2008.

Portfolio margining frees up considerable capital, and many believe it will continue to create greater efficiency in the use of the combined stock and option.

"The whole reason to have margin is to manage true risk," explains Andreas Preuss, the chief executive officer of Eurex. "If you can manage that risk among the entire portfolio, then you not only benefit the customer in terms of freeing up capital, but you do so while continuing just to do just as an effective job of managing risk. Portfolio margining is integral part of the margining philosophy at Eurex, and we are firm believers in its value."

NEW MARKET PARTICIPATION

Changes such as making portfolio margining available help drive new market participation. For instance, portfolio margining is employed by prime brokers[35] to serve hedge funds and others. It stands to reason, then, that the ability to use portfolio margining may make it more attractive for hedge funds to join exchanges and clearinghouses directly. That will give them the same capital savings in the clearinghouse as they would get from their prime brokers.

To understand the differences among market participants, says Krell, "I think you have to look at the individual futures on a one-off basis. I think that there are certain futures contracts—say, futures on indexes—that are very similar to or functional equivalents to the cash market trading. The blurring is less so on commodities such as oil or some of the grains, but more so in the financial futures and continuous use between the future, as the hedging device, and the options. We know that our market participants are active users of

---

[35]A prime broker is one that "acts as settlement agent, provides custody for assets, provides financing for leverage, and prepares daily account statements for its clients, who are money managers, hedge funds, market makers, arbitrageurs, specialists, and other professional investors." (Source: InvestorWords.com, at www.investorwords.com/3835/prime_broker.html; accessed March 7, 2008.

futures, and that's a great thing. The ideal, from an ISE perspective, is if there was the steel index with a future on it, it has options on a future, an exchange-traded fund, a cash-settled option—all of these components trading, including an option on the ETF. They all help each other, and they all work together, so the more instruments, the better."

The Eurex experience establishing a U.S. market amplifies the importance of relationships with market participants. "One of the factors contributing to the outcome of the U.S. exchange endeavor in the years shortly after 2000," notes Andreas Preuss, "is how important it is that you have a genuine and sustainable interest by those who operate the order flow to actually trade your market. Just being an alternative market offerer is not enough. You need a very stable, uninterrupted receipt of order flow for sustained success."

Many consider Jim Newsome responsible for reviving a liberal regime at the U.S. Commodity Futures Trading Commission when he was chairman prior to joining NYMEX. As Benn Steil puts it, the Newsome regime at CFTC "is now widely seen, both in the United States and abroad, as having been a big success, not just in fueling derivatives trading in the United States but in terms of helping to modernize America's derivatives exchanges, which have truly undergone a renaissance in the past year."

Newsome attributes some of the modernization and internationalization of derivates markets, and the success during his period at the CFTC, to regulation. "I was at the CFTC at a fortunate time. The Commodity Futures Modernization Act was an important part of what happened. I think it sometimes gets a bit overlooked. I do not think it was a coincidence that the great uptake in the U.S. markets happened at the same time that the CFMA was implemented. It provided flexibility to the exchanges. It took the regulatory component off the table with regard to business development and business structure. It allowed the exchanges to move very rapidly."

Competition has been at the center of the advances, says Newsome, referring to what Andreas Preuss says about Eurex: "The U.S. exchanges responded very competitively to Eurex's entry into the United States, as you would expect them to—and that helps make a stronger overall marketplace."

THE CFMA AND SINGLE-STOCK FUTURES

In December 2000, President Bill Clinton signed into law the Commodity Futures Modernization Act (CFMA) of 2000, enacted largely to allow the creation of U.S. exchanges that would list single-stock futures (SSFs)—a new kind of derivative. Single-stock futures are future contracts with one particular stock as the underlying asset. When they are purchased, there is no transmission of share rights or dividends. In the 1982, regulators had forbidden their listing on U.S. exchanges primarily because the Commodity Futures Trading Commission and the SEC could not come to an agreement over who would have regulatory authority. After the CFMA became law, the agencies were able to agree on a plan to share jurisdiction, and trading of SSFs began on November 8, 2002.

At first, two new exchanges offered SSFs, but today only one remains. OneChicago is a joint venture between the Chicago Board Options Exchange, the Chicago Mercantile Exchange, and the Chicago Board of Trade. The exchange lists futures on more than 500 stocks, many of them well known.[36] Still, at least in the United States, annual volume in SSF trading continues to lag behind more established derivatives contracts. However, volume has been on an upswing.

There is some considerable controversy associated with the CFMA. Known as the "Enron Loophole," a provision of the Act exempts most OTC energy-derivatives trading on electronic energy commodity markets. The provision got its name because it was drafted by lobbyists working for Enron who were looking to ensure a deregulated environment for the company's "EnronOn-Line" transaction system that allowed buyers and sellers to trade commodity products globally, with Enron as the central counterparty for all trades. The loophole—inserted into the CFMA at the last moment before passage, in the waning hours of the 106th Congress—has helped foster an explosive growth in trading on unregulated electronic energy exchanges.

[36]See www.onechicago.com; accessed March 18, 2008.

The growing internationalization of the derivatives market brings new challenges and complexities. For instance, Newsome's NYMEX is competing head to head with the IntercontinentalExchange (ICE), mentioned in Chapter 1. The challenges are myriad: products that face different limit requirements and different margining requirements because some of what ICE trades is regulated by the Financial Services Authority in the United Kingdom under a different rule structure than NYMEX faces. Should the United States and the European Union intervene to come to grips with such situations as the markets integrate internationally?

Newsome says the regulators are working on it. "That process started when I was at the CFTC," he notes, "primarily through IOSCO. The process is ongoing and is addressing cross-border jurisdictions and how we meld the regulatory structure so that it doesn't lead to competitive advantages. I don't think there is an easy, short-term solution, but I'm confident that the regulators across all jurisdictions are working in a good-faith effort to level the playing field."

THE INTERNATIONAL ORGANIZATION OF SECURITIES COMMISSIONS

The International Organization of Securities Commissions (IOSCO) is an umbrella group comprising all the world's major regulators. The successor of an inter-American regional association created in 1974, it began at an April 1983 meeting in Quito, Ecuador, of 11 securities regulatory agencies from North and South America. The next year, regulators from France, Indonesia, Korea, and the United Kingdom joined. Today the membership is responsible for regulating more than 90 percent of the world's securities markets.

IOSCO's 2002 multilateral memorandum of understanding outlined the group's efforts to facilitate cross-border enforcement and information exchange, and in 2005 IOSCO set out objectives to achieve fair and efficient securities markets worldwide by 2010.

And what of the differences in outlook and approach between the two U.S. agencies, the SEC and the CFTC? As Steil sees it, "The SEC has shown some signs of late of looking more favorably on the CFTC model." He wonders whether the two are converging in philosophy. Newsome thinks they might be getting closer. "But," he says, "I think we're still a long way away."

What about the idea that comes up frequently to merge the two agencies? Newsome thinks it is a terrible idea. "There is still is a huge mentality difference in terms of markets and how to oversee markets. In all fairness to the SEC, that has developed because of the difference in the markets. Also, I think that because the regulatory differences are so great, there would be very few efficiencies in combining the two—the skill set that the CFTC brings to the table is a skill set the SEC does not have, but longer term the SEC mentality would become predominant, and the futures industry would not be well served."

SEC–CFTC MERGER?

Benn Steil and Jim Newsome's discussion of a merger between the Securities and Exchange Commission and the Commodity Futures Trading Commission took place in May 2007. At the time, it was an idea usually put forth by members of Congress and had never gone very far.

At the end of March 2008, however, there was a new call for the merger, this time from the Executive Branch. U.S. Treasury Secretary Henry Paulson Jr. released his "Blueprint for Regulatory Reform" and proposed merging the two agencies. The impetus for the "Blueprint" was the meltdown in the subprime mortgage market and the collapse of investment bank Bear Stearns.

"Having one agency responsible for these critically important issues for all financial products should bring greater consistency to regulation where overlapping requirements currently exist," Paulson said.[37]

Most observers believe such a merger would be tremendously difficult at best and is a nonstarter at worst. One puts it this way: "The two agencies have spent decades skirmishing on the fringes of the financial markets, occasionally reaching accords to divvy up the regulatory landscape. ... [T]he two

---

[37]Quoted in Edward Hayes, "Treasury Recommends SEC, CFTC Merge," CCH Wall Street, Spotlight News, April 7, 2008, at www1.cchwallstreet.com/ws-portal/content/news/container.jsp?fn=04-07-08; accessed April 9, 2008.

agencies have found themselves eyeing each other warily as they've assumed a sometimes-klutzy dual regulatory role with respect to products such as single-stock futures, TRAKRs and publicly traded commodity pools."[38]

The stage may be set for an epic battle, if Paulson's proposal makes any headway at all.

While a potential CFTC-SEC merger plays out, the internationalization of the derivatives markets promises only to expand. Andreas Preuss recalls the frustration of some of the early years when Eurex, which has been a leading light in the internalization of the derivatives market, was first expanding. "We launched in November 1990, but in the first 12 months we did not even manage to grab 3 percent market share," he recalls. "It took us until late 1996 to get to 37 percent market share. Then it took less than two more months to get to 95 percent market share. It was as if we had reached a different version of the often-quoted 'tipping point.' What greatly aided the landslide move was that our ability to offer direct electronic market access to an ever-increasing number of professional market participants made them willing to take on this specific new trading opportunity without a split second's worth of doubt."

EXCHANGES WITH MULTIPLE PRODUCTS

Today that expansion has increased by leaps and bounds. In December 2007, a merger of ISE with Eurex was completed, creating the largest transatlantic derivatives marketplace. With this merger, "Eurex significantly expands its liquidity network into the U.S. and into U.S. Dollar (USD) products. On a combined basis, Eurex and ISE will be the market leader in individual equity and equity index derivatives worldwide."[39]

[38]Matthew Hougan, "Proposed CFTC-SEC Merger Already Derailed?" April 1, 2008, at www.istockanalyst.com/article/viewarticle+articleid_1682524.html; accessed April 9, 2008.
[39]Business Wire, "Eurex and ISE complete merger," December 20, 2007, at http://news.moneycentral.msn.com/ticker/article.aspx?

David Krell explains the decision making behind the merger. "Several things drove that decision," he says. "Exchanges are in the business of product development and distribution. Our feeling was that we would have a far greater reach for product development as a joint business, and far more distribution capability as well. It doesn't hurt us that we have the same mindset about being entrepreneurial and creative and customer-centric. I think that that's very important from a personal standpoint and philosophy about how to run the business. We felt that we could grow much larger, much faster, than doing it alone."

The merger does not only give Eurex an entry into the United States, it also helps ISE expand its business in Europe. "I think the trend is to have exchanges with multiple products, multiple geographies, multiple trading systems, to cater to new audiences. We estimated about 15 percent of the daily volume in the U.S. options business comes from Europe. We think that could be much, much greater if we had a distribution platform into Europe, which is much bigger than the one we currently have. And it's not just Europe; it's the rest of the world as well."

From a Eurex perspective, explains Andreas Preuss, "It has to be noted that of all currently on-exchange traded derivatives, expressed in 2006 numbers, 56 percent are traded in U.S. dollars, 32 percent in Euro denomination, and the remainder in other currencies. Eurex has been pretty much a European currency-focused exchange, with the Euro dominant but also with the Swiss franc. The prerequisites to being a first-tier player are being a multiasset class offerer, a multicurrency offerer, and having multigeography-covering exchanges and clearinghouses. It is clear that a further concentration on one set of currencies, European currencies, is certainly not a way to make a substantial step in that direction."

As for expanding the futures and options business into Asia, Preuss says that there are such ambitions, but that it is complex. "There is a very interesting, very unhomogeneous picture of Asian derivatives markets," he explains. "We will certainly take adequate steps toward building up our distribution capability to be very relevant in Asia. In fact, that is something that is already under way. Today we are already able to connect direct members in a variety of Asian markets. Business from there is developing. I would not want to overstate it at this time, but I think we would probably all agree that it is fundamental to be present in specific marketplaces at the right time to participate in progressively developing volume."

Preuss is perhaps more circumspect when it comes to acquisitions to expand in the Asia region. "Our strategy focuses on creating additional value as efficiently as possible," he says, "and that is driven by the optimal further evolution of organic growth. In certain situations, it could be accompanied by nonorganic growth. We have no dogmatic belief that nonorganic growth is the right way as opposed to organic growth."

Jim Newsome says NYMEX, too, is looking for opportunities to expand. "Different geographical locations our important to us," he says, "because our expertise is in fiscal products. The Dubai venture is an example. The marketplace has wanted a sour crude benchmark for many, many years, and until the government of Dubai created the economic free zone, based primarily upon British law, we had neither the regulatory nor the legal certainty needed to establish a fiscal marketplace there. Now we've done so."

THE DUBAI MERCANTILE EXCHANGE

The launching of the Dubai Mercantile Exchange (DME) underscores the internationalization of derivatives markets. A joint venture among NYMEX, Tatweer (a member of Dubai Holding), and Oman Investment Fund, DME is the Middle East's first futures exchange and the first exchange ever to list contracts for physically delivered Middle East sour oil futures contracts. The partners joined to fill a gap in the world markets: "Approximately 60% of the world's crude reserves are located in the Gulf region, yet there is no sufficiently transparent pricing mechanism for Middle East sour crude oil. The industry has shown a need for a liquid, transparent benchmark for sour crude, and the DME is responding to that need."[40]

In a notice to its members prior to DME's launch, NYMEX hailed the decision by Oman to participate in the market and emphasized its importance. "We are especially pleased with the Sultanate of Oman's historic decision to adopt forward pricing of its crude oil, based on the daily settlement price of the DME's Oman Crude Oil Futures Contract,

Continued

[40]Dubai Mercantile Exchange, "About the DME," at www.dubaimerc.com/faqAboutDubai.html; accessed March 7, 2008.

THE DUBAI MERCANTILE EXCHANGE—Continued

and our consensus of agreement with the Sultanate's Ministry of Finance to acquire a 30% equity stake in the DME. Oman's confidence and support for the DME, as reflected by these recent announcements and the continuation of Dubai's role in this regard underscore the true significance and impact the DME is expected to have on the future pricing of Middle East sour crude oil."[41]

Global Insight, one of the world's leading economic and financial forecasting companies, explained the implications of the DME launch this way on launch day: "[It] will see the start of trading of a new oil futures contract today, seeking to set a new world oil pricing benchmark that is more relevant to Middle Eastern-type crudes. ... If successful, a new price mechanism that better reflects the realities of the world oil markets will be created, potentially revolutionizing the pricing of some of the world's most common crude types."[42]

Middle East oil prices, like other prices, are affected by supply and demand. The DME provides a mechanism for buyers and sellers to transact and manage risk in a market that had not had this mechanism before. "This," argues the DME, "will lead to improved market transparency and price discovery"[43]—all thanks to the internationalization of derivatives markets.

Closer to home, NYMEX also announced a joint venture in February 2007 with the Montreal Bourse to launch an exchange in Alberta, Canada, to trade energy derivatives. Alberta is Canada's oil-rich province.[44] Newsome explains, "We've determined that it's best to enter

---

[41]New York Mercantile Exchange, "Notice to Members No. 107," February 21, 2007, at www.nymex.com/notice_to_member.aspx?id=ntm107&archive=2007; accessed March 7, 2008.

[42]Global Insight, "Dubai Mercantile Exchange Begins Oil Futures Trading Today as New Benchmark Contract Is Sought," May 31, 2007, at www.globalinsight.com/SDA/SDADetail9443.htm; accessed March 7, 2008.

[43]Dubai Mercantile Exchange, *op. cit.*

[44]Alberta Watt Exchange.

foreign jurisdictions with a key partner within that jurisdiction. That's probably the way that we will move forward."

In addition to geographic growth, NYMEX sees tremendous opportunity to continue growing its traditional product base. "But at the same time," says Newsome, "we're looking at new product areas, some related to the energy sector. We just launched the uranium contract, which came about because customers told us they didn't have an efficient method of managing risk in uranium and asked for our help. We were more than happy to do so."

Another growth area is in catastrophic risk. "We're looking very closely at this," Newsome notes, "because the insurance industry came to us about having a futures-tied product to spread that risk among many, many different players. So, we're looking for new product areas very aggressively, and I think our growth will come from both geography and new products."

Might this growth take on the characteristic of blurring the dividing line between the traditional financial futures exchanges and the commodity exchanges? Could those lines even be obliterated? Newsome believes that day may come.

"Traditionally," he states, "exchanges have concentrated on particular product lines. I think clearing is helping blur the line somewhat. We've got the ClearPort system, our OTC clearing component that customers seem to really like; they come to us constantly about problems with clearing OTC products in different areas. So, from our standpoint, the blurring may be led by the ability to clear and shift that risk off of the company books to the exchange."

Trading technology has also been a key to the growth of the derivatives exchanges. The trading technology employed by ISE and other exchanges has attracted financial institutions that had never before seen options trading as a worthwhile opportunity. Krell points to Citadel[45]—market maker and hedge fund that invests more than $20 billion—as an example. "Citadel would probably admit that the ISE was the first exchange they became participants in as liquidity providers. They always participated as hedgers, but we gave them an entry into the liquidity provider marketplace."

---

[45]See www.citadelgroup.com.

Citadel today accounts for up to a quarter of trading in U.S. Treasury bonds but accounts for nothing in the European government bond market. This fact speaks to the way differences in market structure can lead to such dramatic differences in trading from a leading financial institution. In Europe, exchange-traded derivatives volumes still lag well behind the OTC market.

Andreas Preuss explains why. "I believe that the electronic approach taken by specific derivatives exchanges beginning in the late 1980s in Europe has strongly contributed to very deep, very transparent liquidity pools. The strength of these electronic distribution networks—which are in essence order flow concentration networks—is integral to explaining why on-exchange trading, compared to OTC trading, is in a process of catching up."

THE ROLE OF HEDGE FUNDS IN GROWTH

As more hedge funds become direct members of derivatives markets and play a bigger role, they pose some new issues for the exchanges. Jim Newsome believes that the hedge funds are going to be a major component of future growth.

"More and more hedge funds are setting up energy trading desks," he notes, "and hiring energy traders. At this point, the lack of energy traders has made it difficult for them to grow, because it's a relatively limited asset. But they are training traders and growing their desks, and we think they will be a big component of our business. In fact, we think more and more hedge funds will become members of the exchange because as they do more volume, the access to the member rate certainly is a strong financial incentive."

What about political resistance to having hedge funds playing in the commodity markets? This has been an issue before the U.S. Congress, for instance. Newsome believes that there needs to be more education on behalf of the exchanges and the CFTC.

"All of us have spent quite a bit of time on Capitol Hill talking about the role of hedge funds in our markets," says Newsome, "and I don't see that falling off. I think that education process will continue."

Why does it seem as though Congress wants to put on the brakes? Newsome thinks it reflects a lack of understanding. "Hedge funds don't get in and determine the direction of the market," he explains. "They are trend followers. Once they see a direction, they certainly become large participants. But Congress needs to be educated about that process."

MAINTAINING THE LOYALTY OF MARKET MAKERS

Whether it is hedge funds or others, though, a key challenge that all derivatives markets face is to maintain the loyalty of market makers so they don't trade elsewhere. "The most important thing we do at ISE," according to David Krell, "is bring the paper flow to the marketplace, because market makers want to trade not with each other, but with customers—whether they are individual customers or institutional customers. That is a continuing challenge: How do you incent those customers to come to your venue when there are five other places that they can trade exactly the same instrument?"

One question on the minds of many is whether the technology trajectory is such that in 5 to 10 years we could get to options-trading technology that does not require market makers. Could we have a legitimately disintermediated options market, or is that simply not feasible?

From Krell's point of view, it is not a technology issue. He believes it to be a market issue. "On the ISE, we trade options on 1,740 different securities—stocks, indexes, ETFs," he explains. "In one week, we had 154,000 specific options. Every time there is an underlying change in price, all those options have to be updated. It's not like trading in Cisco stock, where you have 20 algorithmic traders on the bid and 30 on the offer. We have lots of Cisco options; we have Google strike prices ranging over hundreds of dollars. On an options market like ours, you don't get all the buying and selling concentrated in just one series. You have this great fragmentation. You have to post the market in each one of them. That requires a different structure than, say, for equities."

THE OCC

One key difference between the futures markets and the options markets is found in clearing. In the United States, the Options Clearing Corporation (OCC) exists as a central clearinghouse for options. As David Krell explains, its origins lie in part in the difference among futures markets, designated contract markets, and securities markets.

"Actually, the OCC was not founded as the OCC," Krell recounts. "It was founded originally as the Chicago Board Options Exchange Clearing Corporation. It became the Options Clearing Corporation when American Stock Exchange filed for trading options and the SEC mandated that all options be fungible contracts. So, when you bought an option on anything SEC-regulated at the CBOE, you could sell it on AMEX. That evolved the OCC into a centralized clearing entity on behalf of all six U.S. options markets. So today, if you buy an option on Google at the ISE, you can sell it in any one of the other five venues, and it will be the same contract that's going to be cleared and settled at the OCC. They're all fungible contracts."

THE OPTIONS CLEARING CORPORATION

The OCC was founded in 1973 and today is the world's largest equity derivatives clearing organization. OCC issues, guarantees, and clears options on underlying assets that include common stocks, stock indices, U.S. treasury securities, interest rate composites, and foreign exchanges. OCC serves a wide range of exchanges, including the major U.S. stock exchanges, as well as other markets trading commodity futures and options and security futures.

As the issuer and guarantor of every options contract executed on all the securities options exchanges in the United States, OCC is the counterparty for all transactions. It is also the only securities clearinghouse in the world to receive an AAA rating by Standard & Poor's. The OCC's importance to the U.S. trading community cannot be underestimated.

Working under both the SEC and the CFTC, the OCC has expanded to clear "a multitude of diverse and sophisticated products. . . . Under its SEC jurisdiction, OCC clears transactions for put and call options on common stocks and other equity issues, stock indexes, foreign currencies, interest rate composites and single-stock futures. As a registered Derivatives Clearing Organization (DCO) under CFTC jurisdiction, we offer clearing and settlement services for transactions in futures and options on futures."[46]

[46]The Options Clearing Corporation, "Who We Are," at www.optionsclearing.com/about/who_we_are/who_we_are.jsp; accessed March 7, 2008.

For Jim Newsome, "The fact that we control our own clearing, and therefore control product launch, is one of the things that has led to a very fast, efficient transformation of the market. We're able to make changes much more quickly and much more efficiently. If that were to be taken away, I think there would be far less dramatic product launches and far less volume growth within the futures sector than we have seen over the last several years."

Fungibility is an important distinction between what we see in the futures markets and what we see in the options markets in the United States. Newsome thinks this should remain the status quo. "The distinction is driven by the difference in the products," he says. "I think the ultimate distinction was between futures and stocks. You get pressure from the banks, in particular, to create fungibility within the futures space."

Differences in the underlying markets are also a factor in maintaining the distinction. "Stock on IBM is stock on IBM," says Newsome. "I think there is much more intellectual property that goes into the development of a futures contract, particularly a physically settled futures contract, not only with regard to the terms of that contract but also the delivery terms. And while we believe it appropriate if an exchange chooses to list and copy that same product, I think it's a completely different step to consider it fungible in terms of trading and clearing."

Of course, intellectual property issues are not confined to the futures business. They are present in the options business, too. "There is much more intellectual property that goes into the development of an options product than a traditional stock," acknowledges Newsome. "But I think recognizing how the OCC developed is one thing. Forcing on options the kind of fungibility that we have in a very mature futures industry is, I think, a completely separate issue."

A discussion of clearing ought to include the increasing importance of state-of-the-art risk management capabilities, states Andreas Preuss. "Whether a clearinghouse can provide that as a service to the marketplace has to do with the ability to control your entire process chain, to not be dependent on having to liaise with someone who is a service provider to you," he says.

Preuss advocates "very strong, integrated trading and clearing solutions—clearinghouses that act in far-reaching competition with each other." This, he says, "will sort of force them to provide to the market the best solutions possible, at all times."

Over the next years, we can expect further improvements in what is already a big, well-established business. "I don't see any end in sight in terms of further improving distribution capability," says Andreas Preuss, "or further improving the speed with which market participants can execute their orders."

Clearly, the future is bright for the derivatives markets. And it's not all about technology.

Chapter 3

Regulation Is Affecting Trade through Settlement

Price and Quantity Discovery

We ended Chapter 2 with the words: "It's not all about technology." Yet the technological advances that have given us automated trading and that have enabled an epic transformation of the financial exchange landscape continue to press forward, raising issue after issue about how the markets function in the new environment.

Two questions arise about the financial exchanges and how they have evolved and continue to evolve concerning discovery mechanisms— questions of prices and of quantity.

Price discovery is the process of determining the price level for a commodity based on supply and demand conditions in the marketplace, whether it is a cash market or a futures market. In essence, *trading* on financial markets is about obtaining prices. When the market is functioning as an "efficient" market, forecasts of future risk and return are the determinants of valuation. The price one observes at any given moment in time in such a market is considered a very good indicator of that future risk and return.

It is, of course, more complicated than that, as readers surely know. That observed price fluctuates as new information is generated. Knowing what to do given new information requires speculation based on a new judgment regarding risk and return. The "speculator" risks capital by taking a position on the market. This process of speculation is what creates price discovery; without it a financial market does not exist.

Quantity discover is something different: the process by which those participating on the market disclose their orders precisely so that they can "meet" each other and transact the shares they want to sell or buy. It can be a difficult process, especially when orders are large.

Primarily, the price discovery process unfolds at a market center such as an exchange. Quantity discovery is more of a backroom function, or it happens within an automated trading system—a so-called "alternative trading venue." But with all the new technological advances, one wonders why an exchange could not provide the quantity discovery mechanism.

Seth Merrin, chief executive officer of Liquidnet, believes it is possible. "But," he says, "you have to figure out exactly what your model is going to be. You can't have a 100,000-share order negotiating with 100 shares, crossing with 100 shares as they do in the upstairs internalization engines."

Russell Loubser, chief executive officer of JSE Limited (previously the Johannesburg Securities Exchange), sees it as a problem of linking all the intermarket trading systems because of fragmented liquidity. "Nothing stops the progressive exchange from addressing exactly that issue," he contends, "and doing it within the exchange. The exchanges perform a very valuable role in price discovery, and the next step is quantitative discovery. Then you've got a really strong franchise."

Does this mean, in effect, having two homes for pricing within one business? Do you need to have multiple entities within one exchange?

"Not necessarily," explains Loubser. "The traditional way of dealing with this issue is to have them in exactly the same exchange but treat them differently. I don't think that's necessarily bad. Even the normal business treats its retail customer different than its wholesale customer—because they need to be treated differently. If you've centralized all the liquidity in one place, then you definitely have a better chance of catering to everybody's individual needs, as opposed to when you have fragmented liquidity and then have the connecting problem."

◼ Transaction Cost Analysis

Transaction cost analysis (TCA) is another area in which the march of technical progress is both raising questions and putting pressure. Transaction costs are a real concern in the financial exchanges business, as the earlier discussion of Project Turquoise and one element of those costs illustrate. The time, effort, and money involved in moving an asset from seller to buyer—including fees—are all transaction costs.

Joseph Wald, cofounder and chief executive officer of EdgeTrade, a New York–based agency-only broker and software development, offers a unique spin on the reason that analyzing these transaction costs matters. "Imagine paying for your groceries and receiving a receipt that shows only the total sum spent, without listing each item you purchased and its respective cost," writes Wald. "Sounds preposterous, yet that's exactly the sort of trade confirmation (receipt) money managers are accepting from many brokers."[1]

Is it a matter of "best execution,"[2] which requires what Wald calls "a complete picture of a transaction's life cycle"? Unfortunately, all

---

[1]Joseph Wald, "Transaction Cost Analysis Provides Important Details About Trade Executions," *Advanced Trading*, January 29, 2007, at www.advancedtrading.com/showArticle.jhtml?articleID=197001380; accessed April 21, 2008.

[2]See Chapter 4 for additional discussion of the best execution.

too often, "Trade cost analysis is left to guesswork, and that's unnecessary when the information already exists."

The remedy, writes Wald, can be found in "details about a client's executed trade [that] is information a brokerage firm already has.... There has to be a full understanding of what is happening on the micro level of a transaction. Without it, a buy-side trader cannot tell how well he might have done, what was missed and the real costs. Transaction cost analysis is only as good as the inputs. But without complete information, buy-side traders will not get the answers they're looking for. And the answers are there."

One key issue, though, has been with the technologies. "The problem with many TCA technologies," writes Larry Tabb of The Tabb Group, a financial markets advisory firm, "is that the models were designed for another age, when the buy-side trader had a limited set of trading options; the majority of buy-side trading was delegated to the broker; and market orders were not shredded into retail-size parcels and executed electronically."[3]

Tabb believes TCA must be implemented across the organization but recognizes that "all trades are not alike and all orders cannot be analyzed using the same criterion." Information must be conveyed electronically to the market from the portfolio manager, which requires connectivity to communicate trading instructions "from the portfolio management system to the order management system to the TCA analytics—and back." Then there is the challenge of timeliness: "feedback needs to occur in real time or daily—at the very least, weekly."

Giovanni Beliossi, managing partner at FGS Capital LLP in London, sees other complications and wonders whether transaction cost analysis ought to be regulator-imposed in Europe through the European Union's Markets in Financial Instruments Directive, since it is part of best execution.

"When best execution is mandated," says Beliossi, "it could be a good thing if it triggers transaction cost analysis." But whether the right tools exist is an open question. "There is no way to measure it.

---

[3]Larry Tabb, "Transaction Cost Analysis: The New Black," *Advanced Trading*, Spring 2005, at www.wallstreetandtech.com/showArticle.jhtml?articleID=60404342; accessed April 21, 2008.

It depends on the way in which the institution or the fund manager trades. It depends on the time horizon of the trade, on the liquidity of the markets. It's like algorithms. Algorithms cannot be used in all markets. They can be used in the fast end of the market and the liquid end of the market, but they're a disaster if they're used for personal caps. They cannot be relied upon. The statistical analysis that is behind them cannot be relied upon. It's the same with transaction cost analysis—a very thorny subject from a technical point of view."

Beliossi and many others agree that it will not be the best thing for everyone to use the same TCA methods. Further, the right benchmarks for performing TCA adequately, though they exist, do so only "in theory."

"The measurement," says Beliossi, "is tricky in that you have to distinguish the various components of accounts in terms of the pricing or the time horizon of measurement. But in our own case, we do have benchmarks that are quite useful. Some are the traditional ones. One is VWAP. There are other, more explicitly benchmark-based ways of measuring the efficiency of trades, such as shortfall or other ways of trading. I think more will develop because of the different nature of the trading we're seeing."

The complications likely explain why, in April 2008, a Tabb Group survey found that "options traders lack the tools to help them quantify slippage and typically rely on simple methods to determine execution quality."[4] In other words, they are not undertaking rigorous transaction cost analysis.

However, reports the Tabb Group, "As the buy side boosts its listed options exposure and adopts more electronic trading tools, it will demand more sophisticated transaction cost analysis (TCA) of options trades.... [It is] the structure of the options market [that] has prevented the adoption of TCA tools that are now commonplace in equity trading.... Additionally, the options market lacks appropriate benchmarks, and the complexity of orders that rely on the prices of underlying assets keeps options traders in the dark. ..."

---

[4]"Options Traders Lack TCA Tools," *Wall Street & Technology*, April 11, 2008, at www.wallstreetandtech.com/showArticle.jhtml?articleID=207200130; accessed April 21, 2008.

That is a continuing problem after the execution of trades. There are other evolution and further challenges at the back end—for instance, in clearing and settlement.

More on Clearing and Settlement

Clearing and settlement, as discussed in Chapter 2, have always been centrally important to the proper, efficient working of markets. In the new world of internationalized, demutualized trading venues, the *post*-trading structure has taken on perhaps even greater importance.

"For many years," says David Hardy, the head of strategic market development for brokerage MF Global, "and I suppose until relatively recently, the post-trade infrastructure was the poor relation." It was a Cinderella kept out of the sunlight in a backroom somewhere, regarded as a necessary evil. That has changed dramatically over the past short period."

Though the exchanges and their IPOs and deals seem to grab the headlines, anyone intimately familiar with the exchanges knows the truth of Hardy's statement and that none of the successful changes that have taken place over the past decade would be possible without the high-integrity support of the clearing and settlement infrastructure. As the exchanges move forward, the decisions that must be made about clearing and settlement all fall within the context of the growing competitive landscape, the business models adopted to face competition's challenges, and the way regulation fits. The latter is especially the case in Europe in the wake of the European Union's Markets in Financial Instruments Directive (MiFID).

Donald Donahue, the chief executive officer of the Depository Trust & Clearing Corporation (DTCC) in the United States, agrees with Hardy that the backroom "plumbing" is more important than ever, at least in Europe. "I'm not sure that in the United States we necessarily would agree that the clearance and settlement infrastructure issues are as much at the top of the mind as they are in Europe," says Donahue. "But they are a central issue in the European dialogue about markets."

One reason clearing and settlement have tended *not* to be a prime topic of conversation, at least in the past, is because "plumbing by definition is boring," according to Donahue. In fact, he says, "It's supposed to be boring, and the only time it becomes of interest is when it is perceived that the plumbing is not working in the way that the markets need the plumbing to work to be able to meet the needs of the markets."

Shift in Focus

That's a pretty good description of why the focus has shifted. Donahue believes the driver to be the European Union's efforts to create a single, unified capital market. It stands to reason, then, says Donahue, "that there are many infrastructure issues—including clearance and settlement—that need to be resolved along the way to that objective."

It should be noted, of course, that DTCC has decided—as David Hardy puts it—"to come over and play in Europe ... because it's become so exciting." In April 2007, DTCC's European subsidiary, EuroCCP, was chosen by Project Turquoise to be its clearance and settlement provider.[5]

LCH.Clearnet is a EuroCCP competitor, and Roger Liddell is its chief executive officer. He thinks there are several explanations for the increased focus on clearing and settlement. "It's not because it is actually more important than in the past," he says, "nor because it has become more difficult. I don't think it has."

What, then, are the reasons, as Liddell sees it? "First of all," he explains, "it's become a lot more profitable. As volumes have gone up, the cost base is reasonably fixed, and marginal costs [have been] relatively low over the last couple of years, the margins that can be made in the clearing process have grown. For many, that has made it an attractive business to be in."

Cast of Characters

The second reason has to do with the cast of characters. As Liddell sees it, "From a customer perspective, particularly for the large broker dealers, the cost issue has in fact become much more important.

---

[5]"DTCC's European Subsidiary Chosen as Clearance and Settlement Provider for Project Turquoise," PR Newswire, April 18, 2008, at www.dtcc.com/news/press/releases/2007/project_turquoise.php; accessed April 21, 2008.

Electronic execution is not just taking place within that community but also in their client base. The market has grown in size in terms of the value of activity that's transacted, but it's grown even more in size in terms of the volume of activity—because of the larger and larger number of smaller and smaller executions. Smaller orders and smaller fills mean that services that are typically priced per unit as opposed to per dollar value become relatively more expensive."

Liddell continues, "Those customers of exchanges look at these businesses in which the margins have been squeezed significantly by pressure from customers on commission rates, but they see that their internal costs of execution and their costs of dealing with client execution have reduced even more dramatically. And that means that the proportion of the overall costs in that business represented by exchange fees—that is, clearing and settlement as a proportion of the whole—is much, much higher. That, I think, is why the level of demand for reduced prices is coming in from customers."

What Liddell describes might appear almost paradoxical: a shift in focus driven on the one hand by customers seeking to get prices down and on the other by entrants seeking high margins.

The backroom plumbing of clearing and settlement was originally designed to serve the infrastructures of national markets. With exchanges consolidating across national borders and with electronic execution the norm, the plumbing that might have worked—to carry the metaphor a bit further—in one house now must work in a consolidated way for the entire street.

Ensuring Competition in the "Plumbing" Business

Dr. Mario Nava heads the European Commission's Financial Markets Infrastructure Unit.[6] The Commission has taken a considerable interest in the "plumbing" part of the market over the past several years, and Nava basically agrees with Liddell's perspective, although from what he calls "the institutional angle."

---

[6]The EU's Financial Markets Infrastructure Unit is described in detail at http://ec. europa.eu/dgs/internal_market/departments/nava_en.htm; accessed April 21, 2008.

Nava first cites the efforts by the commission to develop the Financial Services Action,[7] one of the main components in the European Union's efforts to create a single market for financial services. The Plan, says Nava, "has proved that the European financial markets could do much, much better than they used to and has proved that European financial markets can really serve growth in a dramatic way." But though efforts at the European Commission seem to be focused on establishing a framework that promotes competition while ensuring that the plumbing works well, some wonder why Brussels would not mandate consolidation.

Nava explains that the European Commission has decided not to "dictate" market structure. "If we end up with something like in the United States," he says, "fine enough, if that is the endogenous result of the market. We decided deliberately that dictating market structure would have meant assuming that we bureaucrats know better. We don't want to see a headline in the *Financial Times* that reads: 'Brussels Bureaucrats Expropriate Fantastically Working European Companies'—or anything like that."

Brussels, says Nava, "tends to use the precedent argument, and we have had some quite good precedent. For instance, air transport, railways. In telecommunication, you can make the argument of economies of scale. Why did a phone call from Milan to Paris cost so much? Because you didn't have enough economy of scale. Or you could make the competition argument: If there was a third telephone company other than the Italian or French ones, an independent, private company, prices would go down."

ENCOURAGING MARKET ENTRY

The European leadership, explains Nava, wants to focus on competition that that encourages market entry. To the degree the European Commission intervenes, it is to sort out cross-border aspects, such as interoperability, or inter-industry aspects. "For example," explains

[7]European Union, Financial Services Action Plan, at http://ec.europa.eu/internal_market/finances/actionplan/index_en.htm; accessed March 16, 2008.

Nava, "we deal with CSDs that may try to become banks or banks that may try to become exchanges, and so on. But we feel that the examples from the other sectors are conclusive enough for us not to dictate, *a priori*, that we need one CCP in Europe or any particular number."

In the United States, a centralized model of clearing and settlement has long supported equity trading. Nava's explanation of the contrasting European landscape is confirmed by what seems to be considerable competition for most settlement functions in Europe, along with consolidation across national borders. In the case of Turquoise, big banks are organizing the function, if not actually carrying it out themselves. In other jurisdictions in Europe, one can find a considerable amount of settlement handled by custodian agent banks.

Whatever approach market players are taking, achieving economies of scale appears to be at the center. It is something that can be done with an interoperability bridge, platform sharing among multiple markets, and in other ways. In Europe, where the competitive clearing and settlement model has been embraced, interoperability is critical. Without it, competing organizations cannot function within a consistent market framework.

COOPERATION OR COMPETITION?

One lingering question posed by several clearing and settlement executives is when to cooperate and when to compete. How will economies of scale *best* be achieved? Should Europe embrace a sort of hybrid: a common infrastructure that is operated by and delivered by competing entities?

"It's very, very complicated," says Roger Liddell, "and in Europe I think it is made even more complicated by the different structures that currently exist—some vertical and some horizontal. This is a big problem. When you have this unequal structure, there is a risk that you end up with a lot of competition within the horizontal space and no competition, potentially, in the vertical space."

Is the horizontal model sustainable? Liddell hopes so, but, he says, "Only if we measure carefully the issue of cooperation and competition and don't make the mistake of making the horizontals overly vulnerable while doing nothing to break apart the vertical silos. The right answer, in my view, is to break apart the vertical silos, not to prevent competition among the horizontalists."[8]

Mario Nava, though, does not believe that either the European Commission or even national parliaments in Europe could break apart any of the silos.

To provide one good example of the type of vertical organization under discussion, consider Clearstream. A "leading European supplier of post-trading services," it is a wholly owned subsidiary of Deutsche Börse formed in January 2000 through the merger of Cedel International and Deutsche Börse Clearing.[9] Clearstream illustrates the vertical silo strategy well and has been a moneymaker for Deutsche Börse. In 2006, sales revenues were 700.3 million, representing a 17 percent increase from the previous year.[10]

The United States has largely been the land of the horizontal structure with respect to clearing and settlement. Exchanges certainly did not own majority stakes in these plumbing companies, and what exchange ownership did exist in has been eliminated. Donald Donahue explains why.

"There were a number of drivers, but one is most relevant to this discussion. That is that clearly, with the demutualization of the trading platforms in the States, the dynamics of having an exchange with even nominal share ownership in the clearance and settlement infrastructure were going to change dramatically."

For instance, prior to demutualization, the New York Stock Exchange held—on behalf of its members—just under 30 percent of DTCC's common stock. "With demutualization," explains Donahue, "we knew that how that position got treated, how they would feel obliged to use that position, and so on, were clearly going to change. That was a dynamic we felt that we shouldn't be dealing with. We are absolutely committed

---

[8]See Chapter 4 for additional discussion of the vertical silo debate.

[9]Clearstream, "About Us," at www.clearstream.com/ci/dispatch/en/kir/ci_nav/about_us; accessed April 21, 2008.

[10]"Deutsche Börse sets new record for revenue and earnings in 2006," Press Release, February 21, 2007, at www.clearstream.com/ci/dispatch/en/listcontent/ci_nav/news/30_Press/Content_Files/030_press/2007/press_070221.htm; accessed April 21, 2008.

horizontalists and felt that it was essential to deal with the share owner-ship position to reinforce that commitment to a horizontal structure."

LCH.Clearnet faced a similar juncture, as Roger Liddell explains. But, says Liddell, what LCH.Clearnet did "was designed, quite simply, to make us in principle a lot more independent and in practice to enable us to embark on a different business model where we regulate the level of return and can significantly reduce our prices. That's an unusual action for any commercial organization to take. It's very difficult when you've got a significant shareholder that clearly has a responsibility to its shareholders to maximize the return it can achieve."

What LCH.Clearnet did, recounts Liddell, was to "to use the short-term high levels of profitability to buy back, on an accelerated basis, the ordinary shares owned by Euronext and then seek the approval of our customers and shareholders to change the operating model along the lines that we believed our customers wanted."

Firms like LCH.Clearnet and DTCC "need the support of the user base in order to push through whatever changes they want to make," suggests David Hardy. By contrast, a company like Clearstream has "a different set of dynamics driving the business. It has to look after customers but also has a shareholder base with which to concern itself."

BALANCING NEEDS

One thing all the players worry about is the conflict of interest that could emerge between serving the needs of investors that are seeking the maxi-mum return and the needs of users more interested in competitively priced services. Sir Nigel Wicks says it is a matter of principles. He is chairman of the board of the Euroclear group, "the world's largest provider of domes-tic and cross-border settlement and related services for bond, equity and fund transactions."[11] Euroclear has settlement organizations in France, Belgium, Netherlands, and the United Kingdom and Ireland.

Faced with such a conflict, contends Wicks, "It goes without saying that we would go back to our first principle: We've got to make an ade-quate return for our shareholders. But that principle is based on what is

---

[11]See https://www.euroclear.com/site/public; accessed April 21, 2008.

best for the reliability and efficiency of the market. If you do that, you can solve quite a lot of difficult problems."

With that principle in mind, it is instructive to look at how DTCC came to be involved with Project Turquoise. Donald Donahue takes us through some of the thinking.

"I was listening to a discussion about cooperation versus competition," recounts Donahue, "and I heard a consultant say that when the paradigm shifts, everything goes back to zero. Clearly, there has been a paradigm shift in how Europe is thinking about the market space. We think there is a parallel change going on that is a much more global phenomenon. The NYSE Euronext transaction is a very good example of that."

Here is what Donahue sees happening. "The stitching together of the markets around the globe is a change that is going to proceed much more rapidly than anyone had expected. This means the market space that we are all operating in is not confined by national boundaries. We suspect it's not going to be confined to the Euro zone but that it will evolve to include markets and market infrastructures around the world. For us as an infrastructure in the United States, that means real challenges to establish a position and establish a way of interacting in that larger market space."

THE U.S. INFRASTRUCTURE

What does the U.S. infrastructure have to offer this evolving market space? As Donahue sees it, "We feel that there are very powerful capabilities that exist in the U.S. infrastructure, a level of scalability and a level of resilience because of all the work that was done post-9/11. These are industry assets that can be deployed to meet the objectives of industry members in their attempt to do something in Europe. It is comparable to the periods we went through in the United States in terms of Reg ATS, with the evolution of the ECNs,[12] with the evolution of the automated trading systems, and other shifts. Those are experiences we had 10-plus years ago." Today Europe is undergoing what Donahue sees as the same kind of transformation.

[12]ECNs are discussed in more detail in Chapter 2.

THE IMPORTANCE OF REG ATS

Alternative trading systems (ATS) first emerged in the late 1960s when Instinet provided electronic block-crossing capabilities for institutions. Nasdaq came along a couple years later, and soon ECNs were popping up everywhere. A growing number of ATSs came along to provide proprietary trading systems to a wide variety of market participants. Typically, the Securities and Exchange Commission took no action with respect to these entities—in fact, the "no action letter" was created to provide a mechanism for the SEC to show why it was not intervening to regulate the ATSs as "exchanges."

But by the end of the 1990s, after some 25 "no action letters" related to ATSs, the SEC decided that it did, indeed, need to step in. Regulation ATS, or "Reg ATS" as it has come to be known, was issued in December 1998 to require these small markets do one of three things: They could register as an exchange; they could register as a broker with the National Association of Securities Dealers; or they could operate as an unregulated ATS, so long as they remained under low trading caps.

The importance of Reg ATS to today's competitive landscape in the financial exchanges cannot be understated. In prepared testimony before the U.S. Senate less than a year after Reg ATS went into effect, Jerry Putnam called it "a forward-thinking regulatory approach that recognized the important and unique role of ECNs in the marketplace."[13] Putnam was the chief executive officer of Archipelago ECN at the time and later became a president of the New York Stock Exchange.

Steve Rubinow, chief information officer of NYSE Euronext and formerly a colleague of Putnam's at Archipelago, described it this way in a *Waters* magazine article: "Reg ATS opened the door for anyone who was entrepreneurial and had a vision of how the markets could be different. . . . It opened the door for competition with Nasdaq and the NYSE and all

---

[13]U.S. Senate Banking Committee, Subcommittee on Banking, Hearing on "The Changing Face of Capital Markets and the Impact of ECNs," October 27, 1999, at http://banking.senate.gov/99_10hrg/102799/putnam.htm; accessed April 27, 2008.

other exchanges in a way that hadn't been permissible before—not that people hadn't had the ideas before, but regulations didn't allow them to be implemented—and that was really the beginning of, to quote *The Terminator,* 'the rise of the machines.'"[14]

DTCC serves 10 traditional exchanges and about 50 ECNs or ATS of one kind or another. "That," contends Donahue, "clearly establishes a capability we think is very relevant to the paradigm shift happening in Europe with MiFID. We thought we could provide very real support to the Turquoise investment banks in achieving their objective. And that was really the strategic driver of the decision to go forward. Our subsidiary in Europe, EuroCCP, had been basically dehydrated and put on the shelf someplace for a period of some years. We added water and revived it as a clearing corporation that will provide clearing services to Turquoise."

The decision of the New York Stock Exchange, one of DTCC's largest customers, to merge with a European platform to form NYSE Euronext weighed in the decision as well. "In fact," explains Donahue, "the decision to activate EuroCCP was made before we knew the outcome of our proposal to Turquoise. We have been just as involved in discussions with LCH.Clearnet and with Euroclear about what would happen as NYSE Euronext came together. We've discussed what we would have to be doing both at the clearing level and at the settlement level to support the kind of increasing integration of that trading platform."

The example Donahue gives shows that the emerging model is not exclusively one of competition. "We are going to be collaborating at times," says Donahue. "We may be consolidating at times. We are going to be cooperating at times. And we're going to be competing at times. All of those things."

David Hardy speculates that the appointment of EuroCCP as the Turquoise clearinghouse changes the competitive landscape quite dramatically. How, he wonders, can LCH.Clearnet, Clearstream, and Euroclear,

---

[14]Maureen Callahan, "The Rise of the Machines," *Waters*, January 1, 2008, at www.watersonline.com/public/showPage.html?page=698503; accessed April 27, 2008.

for example, compete? "Can they do it from their independent, horizontal bunkers," asks Hardy, "or must they either collaborate or consolidate to gain the scale of Donahue's organization in Europe?"

Scale and Scope

Another important consideration involves the scope of the customer base for clearing. In the case of a new platform, it is relatively easy to design something to take only transactions that have been executed across it. Buyer and seller are both in the same network, and the service does not have to be particularly intensive. But providing clearing services for a market in its entirety and not only for a small number of very high-volume customers is a different proposition.

This raises the issue of differential pricing. Should clearing prices be the same for all customers? To what extent might smaller customers be disadvantaged if differentials were huge? Is there a risk that the market will become fragmented, with a risk that only the most attractive business could be lost but the least attractive business would always remain?

Those who believe in competition have an answer. As one clearing executive suggests, the lesson to draw from all this is one about scale. The larger players who can achieve scale will take the business, and if Europe cannot get its act together, then Europe will suffer the consequences.

Obviously, scale is important. What about scope? If there is a central counter-party that can clear across classes, does it not create all the benefits of reducing margins? Some wonder whether that is an argument for a mutually owned single entity that clears across asset classes across Europe.

At least "as a conceptual matter," Donald Donahue agrees, "ultimately, that is the direction you need to go. Today EuroCCP is very clearly focused on cash equities, and it's not something that's in the business plan at all. But certainly in the United States, we have our own version of silos. It's asset class silos, not market silos, and it's a problem we are really trying to determine how to adjust. Ultimately, you must bring all these things together."

TARGET2-Securities

If, indeed, it is only a matter of scale, might it not be the case that having a rough equivalent of the DTCC in Europe "solves" the problem? Some wonder whether TARGET2-Securities, a project of the European Central Bank to create centralized clearing and settlement, might be the answer. Others wonder whether the regulatory structure of Europe hampers any effort to create a structure with the necessary scale and that can deliver the needed price point.

TARGET2-SECURITIES

One initiative in Europe has received attention as a possible longer-term model for clearing within the unified European market: TARGET2-Securities (T2S).

In 1999, necessitated by the launch of the European single currency, the European Central Bank (ECB) established the Trans-European Automated Real-time Gross Settlement Express Transfer system (TARGET). It is an interbank payment system that allows real-time processing of cross-border transfers throughout the European Union. Customers of the banks of EU member states, both companies and private persons, can use TARGET to settle trans-European euro-denominated payments. The system speeds up processing.

In 2006, the ECB announced its intention to create a single platform for settling securities in euro central bank money: TARGET2-Securities. The aim of T2S, as explained by Gertrude Tumpel-Gugerell, a member of the ECB executive board, is to "overcome the fragmentation of securities settlement."[15]

Continued

[15]Gertrude Tumpel-Gugerell, "The competitiveness of European financial markets: an economic framework for effective policy-making," *Business Economics*, July 1, 2007, at www.encyclopedia.com/doc/1G1-168218125.html; accessed April 21, 2008.

TARGET2-SECURITIES—Continued

"Despite the single currency," writes Tumpel-Gugerell in the journal *Business Economics*, "EU cross-border settlement costs are much higher than domestic ones; and EU domestic settlement costs are higher than in the United States. [T2S] will provide a single platform for settlements that will create the conditions for central securities depositories (CSDs) to compete to provide the single point of access to the common platform."

It might seem odd for the ECB to take on the issue of securities settlement, but as Tumpel-Gugerell explains, "Market-led initiatives have not led to significant progress in terms of reducing barriers to cross-border trade. It is clear that those benefiting from fragmented markets have little incentive to open up existing national monopolies to competitors. The neutrality of the ECB as a supranational organization with a clear commitment to financial integration and no economic self-interest ensures that a truly Europe-wide infrastructure can be built for the benefit of the users. Moreover, it is common practice for central banks to operate securities settlement systems (and even CSDs)—take, for example, Fedwire Securities in the United States or the BOJ-JGB book-entry system in Japan."

Under the ECB plan, writes Tumpel-Gugerell, "TARGET2-Securities will only be a "settlement platform," whereas the custody, notary, and other functions will remain with the CSDs."

The user requirements phase for T2S was launched in May 2007 and ended in April 2008. On May 23, 2008, the ECB Governing Council issued a proposal to all European CSDs to join the T2S initiative and requested that they inform the ECB by early July whether they intend to use the service once it's in operation. A decision on proceeding is scheduled for later in the summer of 2008, based in part on "the level of support conveyed by CSDs."[16]

The financial markets have not universally embraced the ECB's plan. In late 2007, the "Federation of European Securities Exchanges (FESE) voiced

---

[16]European Central Bank, Press Release, "CSDs invited to join the TARGET2-Securities initiative," May 23, 2008, at www.ecb.int/press/pr/date/2008/html/pr080523_2.en.html; accessed June 7, 2008.

concerns over the cost implications to its members" despite the fact that "the ECB believes the implementation of an integrated securities settlement system in the euro zone could cut settlement costs by up to 90%."[17]

Other criticism has come from the European Central Securities Depositories Association, which sees TARGET2-Securities as a system that "would supplant services currently provided by its members."[18]

Speaking for the ECB, however, Tumpel-Gugerell casts such criticisms aside. "We are convinced," she writes, "that TARGET2-Securities will have a positive impact on competition. In addition, the market will benefit from huge economies of scale on settlement and lower fees for settlement than applied today. This will happen in three ways. First, replacing a multiplicity of settlement platforms in each CSD with the TARGET2-Securities platform decreases the costs of settlement infrastructure. Second, liquidity and collateral needs can be very much reduced by pooling securities and central bank money in a single platform. Third, the possibility of accessing all securities that settle in euros through a single point would reduce custodian back-office costs, owing to the decrease in the number of interfaces. Finally, the customers will benefit from a common settlement service (and price) for both domestic and cross-border transactions. Cross-border settlement will become as efficient as domestic settlement."

The outstanding question is whether T2S is the model for future clearing and settlement in Europe.

CODE OF CONDUCT

In this context, the code of conduct comes up. The European Union created a code of conduct[19] to push exchanges toward interoperability,

---

[17]Finextra News, "FESE cautions over ECB securities settlement project," December 6, 2007, at www.finextra.com/fullstory.asp?id=17830; accessed April 21, 2008.
[18]*Ibid.*
[19]The code of conduct is also discussed in Chapter 4.

and by the end of 2007 more than 60 organizations across Europe had implemented its provisions—"voluntarily."

This discussion of the code of conduct took place before some of the difficulties arose that we discuss further on. But the discussion is instructive, nonetheless.

Mario Nava, offering his support to the code of conduct, perhaps portends some of the difficulties to come. "Is the code a success or not?" he asks. "For the time being, I would dare to say yes. Before the 31st of December [2006], there was basically no information available on prices, services, transparency, and things like that. And now there is."

At least one clearing executive acknowledges that the clarification on price competition, where there is no undue market influences, is providing the necessary confidence to proceed. Of course, as we shall see, the more difficult part of the code was yet to come. That, explains Nava, is "access and interoperability."

In fact, as you can read in the accompanying box, those responsible for establishing the agreement around access and interoperability did meet their deadline. Nevertheless, the tensions that have accompanied the code of conduct since it was first agreed in November 2006 have hardly abated, and as of this writing the problems have escalated to the point where Europe may intervene even further.

THE EUROPEAN CODE OF CONDUCT FOR CLEARING AND SETTLEMENT

As the Federation of European Securities Exchanges (FESE) explains it, "The Code of Conduct aims at enhancing the ability of Organizations to interconnect and ultimately increasing the freedom of choice for market participants. This should be achieved by creating standard unilateral Access between Organizations and Interoperability following the measures described in the Code of Conduct."[20]

---

[20]"FESE—Code of Conduct for C&S—Access and Interoperability," at www.fese.be/en/?inc=page&id=38; accessed March 21, 2008.

The Code of Conduct has three main elements.[21] First, it requires that the signatories provide full transparency for their relevant tariffs and applicable discounts and rebate schemes. Signatories were expected to fulfill this requirement by December 31, 2006.

Second, the code requires that organizations establish the conditions for access and interoperability in accordance with a set of principles detailed in the code. These were agreed and delivered to the European Commission ahead of the deadline of June 30, 2007. As FESE explains, "Europe's trading platforms, central counterparties and settlement systems have agreed a set of detailed Access and Interoperability Guidelines that aim to make the concept of 'cross-border' redundant for securities transactions within the European Union. The new Guidelines provide a basis for the development of new links between these organizations which would offer market participants the freedom to choose their preferred clearing and settlement provider, building on the provisions due to come into effect under the Markets in Financial Instruments Directive."[22] The three organizations involved are the European Association of Central Counterparty Clearing Houses (EACH), the European Central Securities Depositories Association (ECSDA), and FESE, representing many parties.

Third, the code requires signatories to unbundle services and implement accounting separation in accordance with other principles detailed within the code.

At issue is interoperability itself. As Luke Jeffs writes in *Financial News Online US*, "Some bankers argue the code has already been a partial success, by making the pricing of clearing and settlement services more transparent, but compliance with all its recommendations, including the thorny issue of interoperability between clearing houses, was always going to take longer. ... One said: 'The first two principles of the code of conduct—price transparency and unbundling of services—

[21]The explanation of the three elements here is adapted from the explanatory page at the website of SWX Swiss Exchange, at www.swx.com/clearing/ecc_en.html; accessed March 21, 2008.
[22]*Ibid.*

have been dealt with but the more difficult part for the industry was always interoperability. Access requests have been made by clearing houses to other clearing houses but these are going to take longer to set up.'"[23]

LCH.Clearnet and Roger Liddell were at the center of Jeff's article. He explains that "LCH.Clearnet raised the stakes in August [2007] when it issued formal requests to Deutsche Börse, the German exchange, and Borsa Italiana to open up interoperability with those exchanges" own clearing houses, a principle of the code. Last month this tension came to the fore when Roger Liddell, group chief executive at LCH.Clearnet, said: 'Despite the work we have been doing since last August in Frankfurt and Milan, we have no evidence the code of conduct is being successfully implemented elsewhere. We will not, therefore, be prepared to contemplate any further extension of peer-to-peer clearing relationships unless appropriate access is unambiguously established across all the other markets where LCH.Clearnet has sought it. Any further peer-to-peer relationships will only be agreed subject to the clear establishment of appropriate access across relevant markets,' he said."

Whether the code of conduct succeeds is unclear at this writing. But the discussion continues, and if it does succeed—even in a revised form—it will be looked at as a possible model for in other areas beyond clearing and settlement.

EXTENDING THE CODE OF CONDUCT TO DERIVATIVES

Covering only cash equities, one wonders if and when parties might voluntarily agree to extend the code of conduct to derivatives. As Mario Nava explains, "We said from the very beginning that we would like the market participants to extend it voluntarily to all other asset classes, and some have done so. For example, Euroclear extended it from day one—voluntarily to all other asset classes. Still, it is quite a challenge."

[23]Luke Jeffs, "Clearing pact hangs in the balance," *Financial News Online US*, April 18, 2008, at www.financialnews-us.com/?page=ushome&contentid=2450362323; accessed April 21, 2008.

Nigel Wicks of Euroclear is a strong supporter of the code. "If it works," he says, "I think it may be a little time before its benefits actually flow through. I don't think we have a situation where we will have all the discussions, reach agreement, implement the code, go home, and then look out the window the next day and see the market has changed. But just because there are no immediate benefits, no one should think we have to go legislative directive."

Roger Liddell sees success with code, too, despite the concerns expressed in the Luke Jeffs article. "In terms of unbundling, I think it is an unqualified success," he says. "That is a big, big step forward. We certainly welcome it and it's very helpful. An interesting question, though, is whether that should represent a cap or a fixed price. I think all commercial organizations should be free to negotiate arrangements with their customers. Our view is that organizations in the clearing and settlement space should make public what they're doing. They should either publish their price schedule and say they will always apply it religiously, or they should say their prices are negotiable. We have some concerns when it appears that an organization may have a fixed, published schedule but is then negotiating."

Liddell also addresses the question of extending the code of conduct to other asset classes. Can there be the same level of interoperability and open access in the derivatives markets if the question of interoperability of product is not resolved? Roger Liddell believes that there can be access, but he explains, "I think whether the interoperability will be the same is a different matter. I need to see how we end up in securities before I answer that fully."

Liddell continues, "I think the ideal situation is the one that we have in the securities markets in the United States—not in the derivative markets in the United States, where you have a central counter-party that is accessible to all competing exchanges."

What Might Be Next

Introduction

In the long history of financial exchanges, it was not that long ago that the world of exchanges was, in essence, a world of monopoly. At the exchange level, we had a monopoly on liquidity. On the sell side, we had monopolistic access to that monopoly liquidity position. On the buy side, you were absolutely required to go through a broker to access the liquidity and execute a transaction—another monopoly, in a sense.

Where else on the planet, one could ask, or in what other industry could you find a monopoly like that?

This monopolistic environment created a lot of issues and opportunities. On the sell side, it certainly provided a great deal of value because the information players had on the sell side could be used to attract more order flow. And they had a lot of order flow they could try to match. The crossing rates—the percentage of shares executed within a venue versus the number of shares ordered—was actually quite large. Seth Merrin, founder and chief executive officer of Liquidnet, says, "Back in the United States, in 2000, when this was prevalent, we had crossing rates of 30 percent on the block desks."

The requirement that the buy side must go through the sell side made work for a lot of different brokers. The differentiation between brokers was minimal, for the most part. As Merrin explains, "Basically, everyone had to buy and sell the same goods at the same store, so how much differentiation could there really be?"

THE END OF A MONOPOLISTIC TRADING ENVIRONMENT?

This monopolistic world began to change in the United States when competing venues emerged. Institutional Networks (later Instinet) was founded in 1969 and launched the first electronic block-trading capability. Though market share of this and other competitors was minimal, in time their emergence would mean a monumental shift in the world of financial markets. Competing venues in Europe, Canada, and Australia began to siphon small amounts of liquidity from the primary exchanges. ECNs in the United States paved the way and created a template others could use that gave them a credible chance in a competitive environment.

Competitive venues spurred the creation of third-party electronic tools used to access the multiple venues. Those electronic access tools were in the hands of both the buy side and the sell side. The buy side began to feel emancipated. "Once the monopoly was broken," observes Merrin, "the buy side wanted to do it more. The sell side, beginning to feel a bit disintermediated, took the algorithmic tools off their desks and put them into the hands of the buy side. They did it to make sure they could get some access to that order flow."

What really happened, though, is that they hastened the cutting out of the middleman. In 2000, more than two-thirds of all the buy-side order flow went to a block desk on the sell side and was dealt with by humans. Within five years there had been a 180-degree reversal, with roughly the same amount of that flow bypassing the broker's desk.

A development like that, contends Merrin, "changes the entire value proposition between the buy side and the sell side. Today, the sell side does not possess all that much information to give to the buy side—at least that the buy side cannot access on its own. Further, the sell side doesn't have that much flow with which to be able to cross. In the United States today, even the largest brokers have crossing rates of perhaps 7 to 12 percent at the high end, down from 30 percent. Why? Most of this flow is bypassing their desks and going electronically—to be split up, chopped up, and directed to the exchanges themselves."

Once the buy side could execute just what it wanted to on its own, we saw the beginning of agent trade servers (ATSs) coming into the marketplace. For the first time, the buy side has greater access to liquidity than do the sell-side firms. That is tremendously significant, and it took only a few years for this seismic shift to happen. We have gone from a world where the buy side absolutely had to go to the broker to a world where the buy side can actually connect to more liquidity than the brokers, using the same tools. The brokers had to start finding different value propositions.

FRAGMENTATION

Seth Merrin offers what he believes to be a different perspective on the changes and the fragmentation that has accompanied them. "Think about how the buy side works their orders," he suggests. "Their whole responsibility is, basically, to keep control of that order information. That's why they piece out the orders throughout the day. They know that the more information they give out, the more it can hurt them and the more the price starts moving against them. If you think about a buy-side trader with a million shares sitting up on the desk, that trader will give 100,000 shares out to the broker."

Merrin continues, "But the worst part of fragmentation is the 900,000 shares sitting upstairs at the buy-side firm, providing liquidity to no one and with no hope of getting executed. With ATSs and dark pools, what we're doing is reaggregating all of those leftover pieces for all of those traders sitting upstairs at all the buy-side shops, into a brand-new liquidity pool where there once was none. We're reintroducing liquidity that had been fragmented. That is a good market structure development."

It also introduces greater differentiation among brokers—those who are going out to access liquidity for the buy side—where once there was little. A focus on best execution, anywhere in the world, becomes very important, or a focus on the finest research. The model of the past, where the research providers felt that they needed a trading desk, is disappearing. And the major global players want a smaller list of brokers. "We've spoken to many," says Merrin. "Five years ago, their broker list was probably 300. Today, they want 15. Think about any other industry: how many suppliers do you need of the same goods?"

CSAs

One result has been a large increase in commission-sharing agreements (CSAs), now approved by the SEC. CSAs, in turn, accelerate the decline in the number of brokers—a process still under way—and make room for others to capture different flows. More and more, we find order flow internalized with an electronic mechanism, which the SEC requires be referred to as an ATS. No wonder we now find close to 50 different ATSs in the United States, most of which are internalization engines. To Merrin, "That too is a good market structure development, because once you have order flow captured electronically, perhaps we can start sharing it. And that order flow is generally meatier than what's found on the exchange."

An ATS and an exchange are not the same. You can trade anything that you want to on an exchange. An exchange has what Merrin calls "massive breadth but little depth." Conversely, an ATS has "much greater depth but not nearly the breadth of coverage of an exchange." With an ATS, you cannot trade anything you want to. "But," says Merrin, "if you think about ATSs and linking them together and combining and sharing—well, then you have potentially the start of a wholesale marketplace."

Still, there is some way to go. The exchanges, for instance, have always been excellent at price discovery, and ATSs are not. The exchanges, however, have long lacked excellence in quantity discovery. "If you can combine price discovery with quantity discovery, you're servicing all the constituents in the marketplace that much better," contends Merrin. "That, I believe, is going to be the next shift, the next generation of the market structure."

Merrin predicts that it won't be too many years before we see the exchanges and the ATSs combining in some form, with considerable benefits. "It will mean better pricing for everyone."

▌ Consolidation, Collaboration, and Competition

What else might we see in the next few years? The consolidation of the broker industry is on the horizon. Around the world, major brokers are banding together to create competition for the exchanges. They are helping to fuel the move away from the old monopolistic positions by disintermediating the exchanges. "The days of the exchange as monopolies," insists Merrin, "are drawing to a close.

We are also seeing the early stages of the consolidation of the exchange space. New ECNs emerge on a regular basis in the United States. The exchange in Canada has new competition. Turquoise promises to challenge the established order, as does Chi-X.

"I think every exchange needs a competitive exchange," states Merrin. "Competition is going to be good. It might be painful to deal with all these different ATSs, but at some point we'll figure out how to work better together. And, ultimately, it's going to be a much better solution for all constituents."

Per Larsson, chief executive officer of the Dubai International Financial Exchange, believes that there have been more competitive threats in Europe than actual competition. But he agrees that it is coming. "What we will see through value initiatives over the next 5 or 10 years is competition in various segments," says Larsson. "That will create a challenge for both the new initiatives starting up and for the exchanges. The new initiatives will have to choose the right market model to be competitive and to stay competitive over the long term. The traditional exchanges will have to evolve to a more segmented infrastructure, where they offer various solutions for various clients segments—which for the exchanges is a major challenge."

MIDSIZE EUROPEAN EXCHANGES

The midsize European exchanges, such as OMX Nordic Exchange,[1] SWX Swiss Exchange,[2] the Borsa Italiana,[3] and the Bolsa de Madrid,[4] face their own unique challenges. They are very dependent on trading in a handful of Blue Chip stocks. New initiatives aim at reducing operating margins through size, and size is not where these exchanges can grow. To justify their existence, says Larsson, "These exchanges will have to continue to be efficient and deliver value to your existing clients."

Some observers do not believe that Turquoise, for instance, represents a specific threat for the midsize exchanges. More likely, say these observers, any pressure will evolve over a longer term. In time, they will need to provide services more efficiently and provide greater international exposure for listed companies, but for now they can take their time and perhaps look for collaborative opportunities or small consolidations.

[1]OMX Exchanges, a division of Optionsmäklarna/Helsinki Stock Exchange, operates multiple stock exchanges in the Nordic and Baltic countries. The Nordic Market division comprises the Copenhagen, Helsinki, Iceland, and Stockholm Stock Exchanges. The Baltic Market division includes the Riga, Tallinn, and Vilnius Stock Exchanges. See http://omxnordicexchange.com/; accessed January 14, 2008.
[2]SWX Swiss Exchange is based in Zürich. See www.swx.com/index.html; accessed January 14, 2008.
[3]The Borsa Italiana, based in Milan, was acquired by the London Stock Exchange in October 2007. It traces its origins to the Borsa di Commercio founded in Milan in 1808. See www.borsaitaliana.it/homepage/homepage.en.htm; accessed January 14, 2008.
[4]The Bolsa de Madrid, the largest and most international of Spain's four regional stock exchanges, was founded in 1831. See www.bolsamadrid.es/ing/portada.htm; accessed January 14, 2008.

PRESSURE FROM CLIENTS

In May 2007,[5] *The Economist* offered a succinct list of the pressures financial exchanges are feeling from their clients. Attributing it to "a response to a decade of transformation," the magazine quoted Benn Steil, who used the word *obliterated* to describe what has happened to the previous relationships among marketplaces, their users, and the clients of their users.

Pressure #1 is innovation. Because they now "serve shareholders who want to maximize revenue," exchanges must be involved with "streamlining trading, developing new products and selling them widely."

Pressure #2 is on cost. The magazine points to a "sign that brokers sometimes see today's exchanges as foes," namely, "that they have been stepping up their investments in any new marketplace that promises to lower their costs."

Pressure #3 is internalization, "another way in which banks and brokers are circumventing the big exchanges" by "dealing with each other directly." *The Economist* quotes an unnamed exchange head as saying, "The liquidity is no longer in the marketplace. It's on trading desks."

Will waiting be okay, however, or does size really matter? Some observers still contend that it does. They point to the fact that once a trading platform and regulatory infrastructure is in place, and the fixed cost required to put it in place has been expended, profit comes from adding securities to the platform. The growing consolidation in the exchange business through mergers and acquisitions certainly suggests that many see the opportunity that comes from "size."

[5]"Buy, buy, buy: As capital markets expand, the world's financial exchanges are booming and battling for global leadership," *The Economist*, May 24, 2007, at www.economist.com/finance/displaystory.cfm?story_id=9217849; accessed March 3, 2008.

M&A

Martin Graham, director of market services for the London Stock Exchange, explains that the reasons for M&A among exchanges are scale and creating revenue and cost synergies, and that though some are done to drive growth or to internationalize, others are done for defensive reasons. He cites Nasdaq as an example of the latter. Speaking of the LSE, Graham notes, "We already have a very strong international franchise. We're the most international franchise of any exchange, so we don't need to do it for that purpose. However, we will look at any opportunity that improves the quality and efficiency in depth of our markets, drives incremental growth, and enables us to increase value to shareholders."

The New York Stock Exchange took the merger route with Euronext. Olivier Lefebvre, a member of the NYSE Euronext managing committee, sees the merger as providing an opportunity to compete with the London Stock Exchange for foreign blue-chip listings from places like China, Russia, and elsewhere.

"I think that by being the first mover in Europe to attract what historically has been a flow to the United States," explains Lefebvre, "the LSE has taken a very strong position in that field. We believe that combining the visibility, the brand name, and the commercial force of the NYSE with the largest Euro-denominated market is a very good selling proposition for these companies."

COLLABORATION

However, M&A, with all its incumbent complexities, is not the only way available. "One model we're exploring at the moment is the collaborative model," says Martin Graham. "We're working very closely with the Tokyo Stock Exchange. It's the first time it's really been tried. One thing we're doing with Tokyo is creating a small cap market for them. We're also trying to reduce barriers to trade between the different markets and increase both markets' liquidity. And in this model we can share technology without actually getting involved in the corporate transaction." The agreement with LSE is one of several Tokyo has signed with exchanges around the world.

THE TSE: ONE EXAMPLE OF THE COLLABORATION MODEL

The Tokyo Stock Exchange (TSE) is the second largest stock exchange market in the world by market value, second only to the New York Stock Exchange. Established as the Tokyo Kabushiki Torihikijo in 1878, it was combined in 1943 with 10 other exchanges in major Japanese cities to form the Japanese Stock Exchange. Shut down as World War II came to a close, it reopened under its current name in May 1949.

The TSE has, in the last few years, undertaken an ambitious program to build alliances with exchanges abroad. Beginning in the summer of 2006, TSE specifically strengthened its alliances with the Korea Exchange, Shanghai Stock Exchange, Shenzhen Stock Exchange, Taiwan Stock Exchange, National Stock Exchange of India, and Singapore Exchange. Particular efforts have focused on promoting cross-border trading with Korea and Taiwan.

In January 2007, TSE and NYSE Euronext agreed to move forward with a strategic alliance that covers trading systems and technology, investor and issuer services, investment products, and government and regulation.

A cooperation agreement signed in February 2007 between TSE and the London Stock Exchange has resulted in working groups in management and regulation of the markets for emerging companies, mutual listing of new products, and the enhancement of mutual access to both markets.[6] That September, the two exchanges and Lyxor Asset Management announced the listing of the Lyxor ETF Japan on the London Stock Exchange, "giving both institutional and private investors in London access to Japan's most representative index, the TOPIX, for the first time."[7]

---

[6]"Tokyo Stock Exchange Group Annual Report 2007, at www.tse.or.jp/english/about/ir/financials/annual/annual__2007.pdf; accessed January 23, 2008.
[7]TSE News, "London Stock Exchange, Tokyo Stock Exchange, Inc., and Lyxor Asset Management announce listing of Lyxor ETF Japan in London," September 25, 2007, at www.tse.or.jp/english/news/200709/070925_a.html; accessed January 23, 2008.

Olivier Lefebvre takes a slightly different view of collaborations. "I think there is room for corporations' agreement," he says, "but as a complement to M&A, not as a substitute." He cites the complexity of Europe as the reason for his perspective. "What's the problem in Europe? We just have too many infrastructures, too many trading systems, we have too many clearing systems, and so on. It's too expensive to have these vertical silos or transaction chains replicated in every country. We have to rationalize that, and it can't be done with corporation agreements."

How, then, can redundant systems in Europe—and the redundant costs that accompany them—be eliminated? Lefebvre sees two basic ways. "You either put people in bankruptcy through tough competition or you merge and trim down the various systems. We've seen so far that competition is not very effective because there are various barriers to entries."

There will be more consolidation in Europe, as Lefebvre sees it. "If you don't shut down redundant infrastructure," he insists, "you will not reduce the cost to deliver the market participants want. Further M&A steps in Europe are still necessary."

In a world of fully electronic exchanges, the basic product is liquidity. "In liquidity," argues Lefebvre, "consolidation is very important. The network externality of bringing more players to the same securities represents a considerable improvement in the quality of a market. Information technology drives it because of significant economies of scale. At the same time, however, our business is regulated markets, and our clients want to keep their domestic regulation. That's very clear. If clients were not attached to their domestic regulation, they would have opted for different choices a long time ago. The innovation of Euronext was to deliver a fully integrated market by putting together various regulated markets without destroying the home value of these markets. It has worked very well so far."

TRANSATLANTIC MARKET INTEGRATION

Beyond Europe, what are the prospects for genuine transatlantic market integration? Among other things, Euronext is looking at building a clearing link between LCH.Clearnet on the European side and DTCC in the United States. Lefebvre explains what is under way.

"We are looking at two basic objectives," he says, "the first to facilitate, in a cost-effective fashion, the listing and trading of the same securities on both sides rather than through certificates. The second is to interface the systems more efficiently, including at the level of central counterparty clearing, to create more competitive chains to benefit the users but also to improve the competitive position of our exchange. That is an example of where maximizing the value of the users and the exchange are not necessarily contradictory."

Success, of course, depends in part on cooperation from the Securities and Exchange Commission. "Clearly," acknowledges Lefebvre, "regulatory problems exist. The SEC is speeding up a number of new thoughts, though. So we believe that many of the regulatory obstacles might be removed."

Peter Bennett, solutions principal at HCL Technologies and a founder of Tradepoint, thinks the problem could be that the exchanges are spending far too much time trying to buy up their upstart competitors rather than trying to be more dynamic as businesses. "If you're demutualized, you're constantly in play," he says. "This is a huge diversion for any business, let alone an exchange. So that is driving some of the thinking. Then you've got other players who can think of nothing else but who they are going to acquire next to build the huge brand. But it's complicated, and there are a lot of questions to ask. How do you actually consolidate these systems? Whom do you keep and whom do you throw out? How do you move the business forward?"

David Hardy and Tony Mackay take a somewhat contrary view. Hardy, the head of strategic market development for MF Global, sees the conglomeration currently taking place among exchanges as "an opportunity for the next bunch of new kids on the block to come in to shake up the industry some more. That's dynamic and exciting, and whether it's in relation to the cash exchanges or the derivatives exchanges, I think we'll see much the same effect. With legislative changes, particularly in Europe, I'm quite sure that we will see a significant range of alternative trading venues." MF Global touts itself as "the world's leading broker for exchange-traded futures and options."[8]

Tony Mackay, president and managing director of Instinet Europe, believes that the most important thing for Europe is competition among multiple players. "It is more important than consolidation. For investors, what you should have are probably two or three strong competitors that

---

[8]www.mfglobal.com/Pages/default.aspx; accessed January 17, 2008.

compete with each other on price and innovation. We'll all have slightly different business models, and that's great. That's what will drive the competition amongst the exchanges. And then there'll be a few smaller players that go into the darker pools of liquidity. In a few years' time, if competition works and method works, the cost of trading in Europe should come down significantly for everybody. That will make the European capital market deeper and more efficient—and we'll all be winners."

Any discussion of competition inevitably comes back again to the Project Turquoise initiative detailed in Chapter 2. Martin Graham sees Turquoise as a catalyst for very good things and says his London Stock Exchange is gearing up for the competition. "Turquoise will be the first of quite a few competitive initiatives, I believe. It is inevitable that we are going to attract competition. I love competition, because it helps us to force changes internally, and exchanges can be sleepy things. Our job is to ensure we are the most efficient marketplace, the deepest pool of liquidity, with the best, most robust, impressive technology that enables new business to be done. Competition means we must do our job even better. We have continued to reduce costs throughout the market in terms of driving market efficiency, reducing our own costs, our own fees, and enforcing fee reductions elsewhere."

Graham adds an important point, however: that "not everyone likes driving market efficiency." The London Stock Exchange, says Graham, "is moving from a relatively high-margin, low-volume overall marketplace to the other way around. It's all about how you manage that transition. We are very committed to a much higher volume, much lower margin, and overall a lower-cost market. We want to continue to push that."

FEES

The rationale for Turquoise has been attributed to high fees, as discussed in Chapter 2. "One of the things that's driving the banks and the brokers to compete against the exchanges," says Tony Mackay, "is that on a global basis the percentage of our commissions we pay to the exchanges and clearinghouses in Europe is two to three times what we pay the exchanges and clearinghouses in Europe and in Asia.

For such a big capital market, that is quite extraordinary. Essentially, there's a lot of cost that is being sucked out for no return. If we can actually have the total explicit cost of trading in Europe—what gets paid to the exchanges and the clearinghouses for doing almost a utility job—the net beneficiary will be the European capital market."

Graham thinks that with fees "people may be looking at the wrong target," and adds, "The danger of a Turquoise initiative—I can understand why it's happened, and people can see that we've been massively successful and they can create value by doing similar things—is you might turn back time and actually unwind some of those effects [of greater efficiency]." Fragmentation in particular is potentially bad on spreads and could actually massively increase costs for the market."

Peter Bennett wonders why, since each member of the Turquoise consortium doesn't act like an exchange in its own right, because they all have enough liquidity individually to do so. More specifically, though, he speculates about the model Turquoise could adopt. "Will it be the MNS[9] model," he asks, "or will Turquoise simply invent a boring old order book, or might it be a hybrid?"

Philip Hylander, global head of equities trading for Goldman Sachs (one of the investment banks behind Turquoise), answers: "It's likely to be a hybrid market. I think it will incorporate a public limit order book and a nonpublic book as well. I think that it intends not just to look like the current exchanges in terms of its offering."

Hylander continues, "One very interesting area is in terms of the kind of interaction between the internalization that occurs already at broker-dealers and the internalization that will occur there. This would be very positive for the marketplace and something the exchanges would struggle to replicate—namely, that Turquoise, if it structures it right, will be the aggregator of other dark liquidity pools."

---

[9]Multilateral net settlement (MNS) is a settlement system in which payment obligations are accumulated over some specified period, and each settling participant settles (typically by means of a single payment or receipt) the MNS position that results from the transfers made and received by the agent running the system for its own account and on behalf of its customers or nonsettling participants for which it is acting.

INTERNALIZATION

The European Union sees internalization this way: "Internalization means a trading service which avoids stock exchange or alternative trading facilities, allowing the investment service providers to meet their customers' orders for securities listed on the stock exchange from their own account, avoiding thereby the mediation of the stock exchange or the MTF [multitrading facility]. In internalization some other factors apart from the price can also be considered, whereas in stock exchange trading the offer price is of decisive importance. Internalization may nevertheless imply danger if not accompanied by high-level transparency, since in this case the entire market can lose information."[10]

It is a topic of considerable interest, not the least of which is expressed at the U.S. Securities and Exchange Commission. In a 2005 speech,[11] Chester S. Spatt, the SEC's chief economist and director of the Office of Economic Analysis, gave a comprehensive overview of the issues and asked: "To what extent is internalization desirable and when it should be encouraged or allowed? In the trading process intermediaries, such as market makers and specialists, play an important role, especially when there are not coincident arrivals of potential buyers and sellers of a security. Of course, when there are matched arrivals of buyers and sellers the investors find it useful to trade directly with one another and indeed, under such conditions market intermediaries should not undercut the trading dynamics. However, in various contexts intermediaries are able to match the prevailing quote and obtained a desired execution. Of course, this limits the ability of customer orders to directly interact with each other, which may widen market spreads."

[10]"EU Regulations for Listed Companies—Internalization," at www.magyarorszag.hu/english/keyevents/a_vallalk/a_adopenz/a_tozsde/a_tozsdeicegeu20060914.html; accessed March 3, 2008.

[11]Chester S. Spatt, "Speech by SEC Staff: Broad Themes in Market Microstructure," speech at the Market Microstructure Meeting of the National Bureau of Economic Research, Cambridge, Massachusetts, May 6, 2005, at www.sec.gov/news/speech/spch050605css.htm; accessed February 16, 2008. It should be noted that the presentation expresses the author's views and does not necessarily reflect the views of the SEC, its commissioners, or other SEC staff.

Spatt goes on to cite some of his own research with colleagues that suggests "this is analogous to 'price matching' in industrial organization economics and that price matching can be anticompetitive in market equilibrium. For example, firms do not need to quote aggressively if they have the opportunity to match the market price only when necessary to attract the marginal sales. Consequently, in the market microstructure context that means spreads are artificially high."

Admitting that "the empirical consequences of internalization are much more nuanced," Spatt explains: "Many policy innovations have been designed to reduce the extent of internalization of orders and increase the interaction of customers in the marketplace. Benefits to the investing public can arise from both tighter spreads and a reduced need to trade against intermediaries. Measuring the extent to which a customer order interacts with customer orders as compared to when the customer order is executed by an intermediary and assessing the resulting size of the spreads is important to the evaluation of many policy interventions."

Finally, Spatt lists the "range of issues for which attention to internalization is relevant," including "the order-handling rules, payment for order flow, interpositioning by the specialist, auto-quoting and the ability of the specialist to stop the market, market fragmentation, market data revenues, dealerization of the bond market, price improvement programs ... and the definition of an 'exchange.'"

Later, Mark Sobel, U.S. deputy assistant secretary of the treasury for international monetary and financial policy, gave a speech on the "U.S.-EU Financial Dialogue" and spoke of internalization as a topic to keep an eye on. Referring to the Markets in Financial Instruments Directive (MiFID), Sobel said: "Some European countries required that any securities trading take place on exchanges—the so-called 'concentration rule.' Others allowed firms to 'internalize' transactions, a practice familiar in the U.K. and the United States. In the end, after much debate, a delicate compromise was reached allowing 'internalization' throughout the EU and putting the 'concentration rule' aside. This was progress. Not surprisingly, since then there has been continued active discussion about the conditions under which internalization could take place. The U.S. side has monitored this debate. The devil lies in the details.

Continued

> ### INTERNALIZATION—Continued
>
> We stressed in the Dialogue that the goal is about rewarding innovation and allowing regulation to support different market practices in a neutral manner and that the terms under which internationalization is permitted are critical for the future vibrance of European financial markets. Brussels agrees."[12]

Does internalization represent another competitive threat? Hylander says that what he describes above "doesn't need Turquoise to happen." He explains, "There are already discussions about bilateral access to liquidity pools, individual broker dealers having agreements with other broker dealers. But that is a very complex negotiation, and the game theory around who you would agree to offer bilateral access to is very complex, too. It's much easier to see how that could be sorted out within a Turquoise framework. It wouldn't be free from problems, but it would be much easier to see how that would operate. It is even conceivable that some people may forego internalization at their own firms for internalization within some kind of industry solution, be it Turquoise or another."

METHOD

As Xavier Rolet, the managing director for Lehman Brothers Europe, sees it, "We're moving from a fragmented environment, essentially exchange-dependent, to an environment where the exchange retains a central position but in which wholesale market makers can bring about additional efficiencies—thanks to method, including systematic internalization. But for wholesale companies to take matters in their own hand and create a separate exchange structure potentially threatens the

[12]Mark Sobel, "Finding Common Ground: Inside the U.S.-EU Financial Dialogue," speech at the European Union Studies Center, Graduate Center, City University of New York, New York City, March 9, 2006, at http://useu.usmission.gov/Dossiers/Financial_Services/Mar0906_Sobel_Financial_Dialogue.asp; accessed February 16, 2008.

regulatory 'cover' that is provided by method. Whether the initiative succeeds or not—and given all the firepower one would expect Turquoise to be wildly successful—it raises questions around method and whether the power of some wholesale traders may not be excessive. We're a little bit worried about that."

From Martin Graham's perspective, there are some potential conflicts of interest. "I am concerned about the potential conflict between best execution and trying to route orders to different platforms. How those things are managed is a difficult question. I think I can understand why Turquoise has emerged, and if it actually does provide great market efficiency, then it will grow the overall size of the market and everyone will benefit. But I don't think all the people involved in Turquoise necessarily have a market efficiency goal, and some of the unintended consequences—or maybe intended consequences of Turquoise—could actually be quite damaging for the market."

Benn Steil of the Council on Foreign Relations notes that there seems to be a split perception among banks about method, which plays into this very issue. "On the one hand," he says, "there's the opportunity created by method to compete with the exchanges. Now that the concentration rules[13] have been eliminated, the banks have more discretion about where to send their orders. So, it does clearly provide this powerful mechanism to compete with the exchanges, and to use discretion about where to send order flow. On the other hand, I've heard lots of complaints about the cost that method imposes on banks, particularly the pre-trade transparency requirements, Project Boat is one way to try to get a grip on those costs by building a consortium to deal with the question."

PROJECT BOAT

In the latter half of 2006, a consortium of nine investment banks announced that they would team up to create a single trade and market data dissemination platform to meet the demands for pre- and post-trade transparency embedded in the Markets in Financial Instruments Directive that came into force on

Continued

---

[13]See the earlier box on "Internalization" (page 114).

PROJECT BOAT—Continued

November 1, 2007. Notably, the consortium nearly replicates (though not exactly) the group that originally came together for Project Turquoise.[14]

MiFID makes it permissible for these banks to form their own trade reporting authority and charge for disseminating their own market data. Previously, traders executing off-exchange had been required by some markets to report those trades to exchanges, which would in turn charge a fee to receive and distribute the data. Boat is intended to create a single pan-European platform for reporting those trades.

Writing in *Waters* magazine,[15] Joel Clark says, "Although success cannot be guaranteed, Boat may have more going for it than Turquoise." One reason is that it is easier to accomplish technologically. But, Clark adds, "Boat could face stormier seas if more initiatives and trading facilities spring up"—which is something MiFID allows.

By the middle of 2007, with the implementation date for MiFID nearing, more banks signed on. "Barclays Capital, BNP Paribas, Dresdner Kleinwort, JP Morgan and Royal Bank of Scotland have all selected Project Boat to provide its pre- and post-trade reporting requirements under [MiFID]," reported *OpRisk & Compliance* magazine.[16]

After MiFID's implementation, Reuters reported in January 2008 that the nine banks that set up Boat would sell their stakes in the project to the data vendor that operates the platform, Markit. Reuters also noted the effect Project Boat had had on the competitive landscape. For example,

---

[14]The nine banks in the consortium are ABN Amro, Citi, Credit Suisse, Deutsche Bank, Goldman Sachs, HSBC, Merrill Lynch, Morgan Stanley, and UBS. BNP Paribas and Société Générale, both Turquoise founders, are not among the group. ABM Amro and HSBC are not among the Turquoise founders.

[15]Joel Clark, "MiFID High Tide: Will Project Boat and similar initiatives sail smoothly in post-MiFID waters?" *Waters*, August 1, 2007, at http://db.riskwaters.com/public/showPage.html?page=461894; accessed February 16, 2008.

[16]Victoria Pennington, "As Mifid-day inches closer, Project Boat gains adherents," *OpRisk & Compliance*, June 12, 2007, at www.opriskandcompliance.com/public/showPage.html?page=453208; accessed February 16, 2008.

"London Stock Exchange, which offers a similar service, had slashed its trade-reporting fees by 80 percent when [MiFID] became effective." Further, Reuters said, "More than 22 investment houses now use Boat to meet their over the counter equity reporting obligations required by MiFID."[17]

From Russell Loubser's perspective, competition—in whatever form it might take—is going to shake out the overall exchange business, and that it's the newer players that are most likely to suffer. Loubser is the chief executive officer of JSE Limited (previously the Johannesburg Securities Exchange), Africa's largest stock exchange.

"I would venture to say that there are a number of new boys and girls that won't be around next year," says Loubser. "By the same token, the old established businesses will still be around in 10 years. Everything comes down to the people who run those businesses. Put the wrong people in young businesses, and they'll disappear. If you've got the wrong people in old businesses, they will disappear. If the old exchanges start doing things differently, they'll stick around."

VERTICAL SILOS

One of the biggest debates playing out in the context of consolidation and competition is the debate over vertical silos. Views of the vertical silo question abound, and the history of vertical silos in Europe is not without its twists and turns. Martin Graham of the London Stock Exchange, while acknowledging that vertical silos in the short term "give you the ability to control market structure, which helps shareholders," states emphatically: "We do not like vertical silos. They have some significant potential incentives for anticompetitive behavior."

Olivier Lefebvre of NYSE Euronext concurs with Martin Graham. "We are totally against vertical silos in the field of securities," he states.

---

[17]Reuters, "Banks to Sell Stake in Boat to Markit—Sources," January 21, 2008, at www.reuters.com/article/bankingFinancial/idUSL2141879320080121; accessed February 16, 2008.

"We believe that the approach of Commissioner McCreevy is, in principle, the right approach. Maintaining vertical silos is clearly a barrier to entry, one way or another."

In Europe, as of this writing, regulators have been pushing exchanges toward "interoperability" as a way of deconstructing the vertical silos, and Charlie McCreevy, the European Union's internal markets commissioner, has warned against "endless foot-dragging" by providers of clearing and settlement services for the stock exchanges. Having established a code of conduct on interoperability in 2006 that relied on voluntary cooperation, McCreevy is looking at compliance as a "last chance."[18]

Agreeing with McCreevy, however, could have an undesirable side effect for Olivier Lefebvre. "We have to be very aware that the result of this might be paradoxical in terms of effectively increasing competitive pressure," he explains. "We might be in a situation where it is designed to unbundled the silos or at least to open them, in effect, but the rest might be too weak."

THE VERTICAL SILO DEBATE

Traditionally, some exchanges sought to protect themselves from outside competition by building so-called "vertical silos" in which they integrate the trading and settlement platform—in essence, owning the front and back ends of trading. It is a vertical silo that the Chicago Mercantile Exchange has now constructed for itself.

Craig Pirrong, a professor at Bauer College of Business at the University of Houston, provides a good, succinct explication of the vertical silo debate. "The primary objection to the 'vertical silo' model of financial trading," he writes, "is that due to the substantial scale and scope economies in clearing, an exchange integrated into all three functions can deny access to its clearing and settlement facilities to foreclose entry by another firm offering execution services in the products traded on the integrated

---

[18]Nikki Tait and Jeremy Grant, "EU threat on clearing services," *Financial Times*, April 20, 2008, at http://us.ft.com/ftgateway/superpage.ft?news_id=fto042020081830369834; accessed April 22, 2008.

exchange. It has long been understood, however, that vertical integration can also be an efficient way to organize transactions, because it can eliminate double marginalization, mitigate holdups, and provide superior incentives to invest in specific assets."[19]

Over the years, many challengers have come along to confront the vertical silos, and it is notable that—at least to some degree—the tables seem to have been turned. Some of the national exchanges in Europe are today the most vociferous opponents of vertical silos. It could well be because the investment banks that are constructing Turquoise[20] have come up with the competitive solution that has long been elusive.

Consider just one example of the raging debate. The chief executive of the London Stock Exchange, Clara Furse, warned in April 2008 of a "domino effect" of spreading anticompetitive behavior unless regulators in Britain intervene and force competition in the exchange clearing business. Writing in the *Financial Times*, Furse expressed concern that the vertical silo model was being introduced by exchanges in Europe and specifically criticized the plan by ICE and Liffe to establish their own clearing operation in London.[21]

The chief executive of Euronext.Liffe, Hugh Freedberg, hit back, contending, "If Liffe is not able freely to choose its clearing solution, it would not be able to compete on a level playing field and would be at a competitive disadvantage."[22]

Continued

---

[19]Craig Pirrong, "The Industrial Organization of Execution, Clearing and Settlement in Financial Markets," January 23, 2007; available for download from the International Society for New Economics at www.isnie.org/assets/files/papers2007/craig.pdf; accessed March 16, 2008. The three functions to which Pirrong refers are those in his paper's title.

[20]Turquoise is discussed in detail in Chapter 2.

[21]"Furse calls for regulators to intervene on vertical silos," at www.finextra.com/fullstory.asp?id=18348; accessed April 22, 2008.

[22]Luke Jeffs, "Liffe counters complaints against clearing plans," Financial News Online US, at www.financialnews-us.com/?page=ustradingtechnology&contentid=2450417914; accessed April 22, 2008.

THE VERTICAL SILO DEBATE—Continued

The arguments might seem, to some, disingenuous. After all, reports Financial News Online US, "The LSE has considered launching its own clearing house" based on the Italian clearinghouse owned by Borsa Italiana, which "the LSE bought in October [2007]." While a spokesperson admitted that Borsa Italiana "is organized vertically," she insisted that it "does not operate as an exclusive silo." Meanwhile, an exchange analyst at broker MF Global, Mamoun Tazi, said of the LSE, "They seem to be overlooking the fact that they own their own vertical silo in Borsa Italiana."[23]

Russell Loubser's perspective from South Africa is to warn against generalization. "I think you can run a horizontal situation very badly and you can run a vertical situation very badly, and the opposite also applies. I think people should reserve their judgment until they understand the specific circumstances in a particular situation."

Describing the South African situation, Loubser says that if the stock exchange had not taken a leading role in pushing the dematerialization of equity scrip,[24] the progress the JSE achieved to date might not have come to pass. "As a result," he explains, "we have a vertical silo. It's easy to say now it should be horizontal now that it's making a lot of money. But 10 years ago, nobody wanted to touch that thing. Everybody said to go the vertical route because they knew we were funding it."

Innovation and Product Development

As consolidation and collaboration expand and as new competing venues emerge, important players are working overtime to innovate and develop new products for the financial exchanges. Process is a

---

[23]Luke Jeffs, *ibid.*

[24]In May 1996, the Johannesburg Stock Exchange signed a "Memorandum of Understanding" with banks to establish Share Transactions Totally Electronic (STRATE), an electronic settlement system for the equities market in the country. This was enabled by eliminating physical stock certificates ("dematerialization") and establishing an all-electronic system of bookkeeping in a Central Securities Depository.

key area for innovation. "There are all sorts of different trading styles," explains Peter Bennett, "and for each trading style, you need a different process. But there has been very little innovation in terms of the process. It's a huge scope for innovation, and I don't see it coming from the incumbent exchanges."

In terms of new products, the possibilities can appear limitless. Bennett mentions carbon credit trading, and wonders why British farmers who want to participate in a carbon market must access it in the United States. "Where is the London Stock Exchange? Where is anyone in Europe providing a carbon credit exchange? How can we miss that?"

JOHANNESBURG STOCK EXCHANGE

In South Africa, Russell Loubser's JSE Limited has shown that product development is still alive and well with the creation of an agricultural commodities market—turning on its head the conventional wisdom that regional derivatives markets in agriculture are impossible and that these products can be traded only in the United States. "We started that market in 1995," notes Loubser. "Nobody gave it a chance. Now we have a very vibrant agricultural futures exchange in South Africa."

In addition, JSE created an alternative market for small and medium caps and introduced single stock futures. After only a few years, the exchange became the world's largest venue for SSFs as measured by trading volume. "SSFs have become the preferred entry point into South African [equities]," according to Allan Thomson, JSE director of trading.[25] At the London Stock Exchange, Martin Graham says, steps have been taken to expand product offerings in a retail context.

These are a few examples of exchange officials taking an interest in doing the right thing. "I always come back to the same issue," says Russell Loubser. "It depends entirely on the quality, experience, motivation, and passion of the people running the business. If you have the wrong people, you have no hope. If you have the right people, you may still have no hope, but at least you've got a chance."

[25]Doug Cameron, "Single-Stock Futures Boom in South Africa, Languish in US," Dow Jones Newswires, at http://news.morningstar.com/newsnet/ViewNews.aspx?article=/ DJ/200804091715DOWJONESDJONLINE001058_univ.xml; accessed January 17, 2008.

A New World for Private Shareholders

All the progress over the past decade has changed the markets and the big players—the hedge funds, institutional investors, pension funds, and so on—but the revolution has also created a new world for private shareholders. Today the individual investor pays lower fees and has greater market access than ever before.

Olivier Lefebvre speaks of this in a European context. "In all European markets, as an individual you pay more once you buy a foreign share relative to a domestic share. On Euronext, the cost of trading for individuals has been harmonized to the domestic level for all shares. In addition, there is a general trend in Europe where market quality has improved in terms of spread reduction—by an additional 20 percent. Studies show that this is also an effect of the integration of the Euronext market on the spread. I think these are very practical examples that show that for an individual investor, the accessibility of a larger range of instruments has improved in terms of cost of trading, but even in the domestic market there has been an improvement linked to the integration."

At the London Stock Exchange, things have changed for the individual investor as well. As Martin Graham explains, "We've been working very actively to help promote direct market access to retail, because that will enable retail to reduce its overall cost of trading, particularly the spread cost. We now have three or four providers of direct market access so retail can actually interact with the professional market, and we're working on some quite significant strategies to make sure that happens in a more pervasive manner."

LSE has also seen a proliferation in exchange-traded funds and exchange-traded commodities that give retail access to different asset classes. "You can buy Taiwanese equities or European property," says Graham. "You can buy hogs and all sorts of things because of what we've done." Down the road, the LSE wants to improve access even more and expand the range of products.[26]

---

[26]One issue Graham mentions that requires more discussion than is possible here is "stamp duty"—a form of tax charged in the United Kingdom on the transfer of shares and securities that can be onerous for investors.

EDUCATING INVESTORS

To capture all the opportunities of a retail market, though, there is much more to do than simply expanding access and products. Private investors need to be educated, too.

Writing in his regular column in the May 2007 issue of *Trading Places*, Patrick L. Young decries the state of exchange education, which "has yet to leave the dark ages." He goes on to argue, "Education is a stealth concept" and states, "A key future step for exchanges is to enhance mass adult financial investment literacy from its current pre-Stone Age point. Serious progressive thinking is required for financial education."[27]

Perhaps education is not a critical issue for the wholesale market, but how important to the future of the exchanges is advancing the level of education among private investors? Mary Schapiro, chief executive officer of the U.S. Financial Industry Regulatory Authority (FINRA), agrees that "the state of financial literacy, at least in the United States, is very poor." And, she says, "When you couple that with the fact that we have an aging population woefully unprepared financially for retirement, we have a tsunami of problems out there about to roll over us."

At least in the United Sates, Schapiro sees a role for regulators here. "We actually have a very large investor education foundation," she says, "the largest in the United States dedicated just to investor education. We work very hard to fund research and give grants to develop wonderful content and survey investors and understand how to reach them most effectively and when. But the real issue is: How do you do distribution through a country the size of the United States that's effective and reaches people—whether it's through primary and secondary education, the library system, on-the-job training. We're trying to find the right ways to reach different segments of our population with a great content that some we've developed, but much has been developed by the industry or by others."

---

[27]Patrick L. Young, "Education by Stealth," *Trading Places*, Issue 19, May 2007, at www.mondovisione.com/index.cfm?section=tp&action=detail&id=67051; accessed April 24, 2008.

SIMPLIFICATION

Luis Correia da Silva, managing director and joint CEO of Oxford Economic Research Associates (Oxera), agrees that educating at the retail level is important but also suggests some other things that need to be done. "There is room," he contends, "for simplifying products and for simple metrics for measuring performance. There is also room for regulation to develop ways to minimize the agency problems between the intermediaries acting on behalf of the investors and the retail investors. Those are the things we need on the retail side: metrics, simplification of products, and minimizing conflicts of interest."

Mary Schapiro would like to see some simplification, as well, in a different area. "Regulators need to get our disclosure regime under control," she says. "When we have a problem, we write a rule that says you must disclose this because it's a problem. Over the years, we've created a disclosure system with so much detail that investors can no longer find out what's important. Mutual funds are a great example. It's a phenomenal product for most investors, but they get a prospectus and a statement of additional information at the time of sale, not before. It's virtually useless to them. We must get a handle on the voluminous disclosure that we require that really doesn't benefit investors in any way."

▌ New Technology Frontiers

The growing will to open the markets to greater access across the board would go nowhere without the technological advances that are making it possible. We have discussed many of these advances in these pages. With the increased access they provide comes a full-frontal assault on one of the things that matters most in the world of electronic trading—*latency.*

LATENCY

Put simply, latency is the amount of time that elapses between the initiation of a trade and its completion (or response to it). In a swift and high-stakes world of finance, milliseconds matter. One approach under discussion to cut latency is for exchanges to provide hosting services to some of the largest traders. The technological challenges are substantial. How do you speed things up on an exchange already handling more than 100,000 transactions while ensuring optimal data analysis and routing? Can the best execution be assured at the "speed of light" or beyond?

We can offer no consensus answer. Part of the answer has to do with the framework for best execution. Traditionally, *best execution* has meant executing a trade at the best price under the circumstances, with execution price and speed as very important—but not the only—factors.[28] In the United States, some argue, *best execution* focuses on latency almost to a fault. Others wonder whether best execution on a global scale will evolve into being described more specifically in terms of how *child order* of larger *parent orders* go through the exchanges. In any case, technology is sure to drive the definition.

Philips Hylander of Goldman Sachs is sure that latency will *not* be the only factor in characterizing best execution. Further, he doesn't believe it will be the "sole vector on which we'll compete."[29] Argues Hylander, "Not all liquidity is driven by each incremental microsecond of liquidity. There will be situations where people feel they can sacrifice latency in order to spread capture."

TRADING FASTER THAN THE SPEED OF LIGHT

"In the time it takes to bat your lashes," wrote Joshua Boak of *The Chicago Tribune*, "the Chicago Mercantile Exchange executes and clears 33 electronic trades. That velocity, a trade every 15 milliseconds, can leave anyone who relies solely on eyesight blind to what's happening in the markets."[30]

Continued

[28]For instance, the Markets in Financial Instruments Directive (MiFID) of the European Union, in Article 21 ("Obligation to execute orders on terms most favourable to the client"), states that "best execution" not only takes price into account, but also "costs, speed, likelihood of execution and settlement, size, nature, or any other consideration relevant to the execution of the order." See www.markets-in-financial-instruments-directive.com/Article21.htm; accessed March 3, 2008.

[29]Add note when query re: citing speakers is resolved.

[30]Joshua Boak, "Globex: Upping the Ante in the Electronic Trading Wars," January 29, 2008, at www.technewsworld.com/story/61422.html; accessed March 9, 2008.

TRADING FASTER THAN THE SPEED OF LIGHT—Continued

Boak was describing CME's Globex electronic exchange, which recorded 1.33 billion deals in 2007 and generated about $825 million in revenue. He goes on to write, "As prices shifted several times a second in volatile trading ... the Chicago Board Options Exchange routed 118,000 messages a second." That "burst of traffic overloaded the centralized options-price-reporting authority, shutting down the New York Stock Exchange electronic options program for approximately 10 minutes and the American Stock Exchange for about an hour, while the CBOE continued processing trades."

Phil Slocum, the CBOE executive vice president of trading operations, describes it as a "technology war" and adds: "And how fast you can go is how you wage that war."

For the CME Group, there are tremendous financial stakes. "Faster speeds translate into higher volumes, producing more fees. ... As the time for completing a trade dropped from 600 milliseconds in 2003, the Merc's volume on Globex grew fourfold. The volume fueled a 33 percent increase in 2006 net income, to US$407 million."

In *Waters* magazine, Emily Fraser contends, "The speed of market data dissemination is now so fast that the only way a firm can reduce market data latency any further is to actually share datacenter floor space with the exchanges themselves."[31]

Fraser reports that one anonymous respondent to a survey conducted by Inside Market Data in 2007 stated that the "tolerable latency within the New York metro area is currently 10 to 12 milliseconds, and as many as eight of those precious milliseconds are taken up by exchange or ECN dissemination. Since the speed of light is the ultimate limitation, the further a firm is from the exchange, the longer it takes for data to be delivered."

[31]Emily Fraser, "Close to You," *Waters*, October 1, 2007, at www.watersonline.com/public/showPage.html?page=478203; accessed March 9, 2008.

In article after article and analysis after analysis over the past couple of years, those three words—*speed of light*—have become the measure by which conquering latency seems to be defined.

Richard Martin, reporting in *InformationWeek*, echoes Fraser's description of firms using physical proximity to overcome technical barriers. "A 1-millisecond advantage in trading applications," writes Martin, "can be worth $100 million a year to a major brokerage firm, by one estimate. The fastest systems, running from traders' desks to exchange data centers, can execute transactions in a few milliseconds—so fast, in fact, that the physical distance between two computers processing a transaction can slow down how fast it happens. ... To overcome it, many high-frequency algorithmic traders are moving their systems as close to the Wall Street exchanges as possible."[32]

Calling the data-latency race "the spear point of the global movement to eradicate barriers—geographic, technical, psychological—to fair and transparent markets," Martin cites BATS Trading founder David Cummings' prediction that high-speed automated trading over electronic networks will eventually make the traditional obsolete or nearly obsolete.

Where will it all end? Richard Martin describes BT Radianz and its Ultra Access service that "provides sub-1 millisecond order-routing services between traders and exchanges in the New York area"—which is "as fast as you can get." After that, according to BT's chief technology officer, Mark Akass, "You get to the speed-of-light limitation. ... There's not a lot you can do in terms of getting faster."

Larry Tabb of The Tabb Group, a financial markets advisory firm, described a focus group on connectivity he hosted in late 2004. "[W]e brought in some of the best and brightest industry connectivity specialists. What they said surprised me. They basically said that 'the speed of light is too slow.' They noted that firms located further away from the market

Continued

---

[32]Richard Martin, "Wall Street's Quest to Process Data at the Speed of Light," *InformationWeek*, April 21, 2007, at www.informationweek.com/story/showArticle. jhtml?articleID=199200297; accessed March 9, 2008.

> **TRADING FASTER THAN THE SPEED OF LIGHT—Continued**
>
> center were being shut out because the speed of light could not carry their orders to market fast enough."[33]
>
> "If anybody knows how to get a signal transmitted faster than the speed of light," David Cummings told Martin, "I'd like talk with them."

Of course, as we go forward, the uncertainty of technological change and the innovative spirit among market players teaches us that prediction is a roll of the dice. As one observer has said, "The wonderful thing about competition is this: Turquoise can have the greatest technical minds in the world, Instinet can have the history with Chi-X, but there are always people out there who will build faster connections to suit their model. And in an open framework, we're all winners."

---

[33]Larry Tabb, "Light Speed and The Buttonwood Tree," *Wall Street and Technology*, January 5, 2005, at www.wallstreetandtech.com/showArticle.jhtml?articleID=56900894; accessed March 9, 2008.

About the Author

Herbie Skeete is the founder and managing director of Mondo Visione, publisher of specialist exchanges information, and organizer of the Mondo Visione Exchange Forum. With over 25 years experience in the financial information industry, Skeete is recognized globally as an expert on exchanges and content issues.

Since 1991, he has produced the industry-standard *Handbook of World Stock, Derivative & Commodity Exchanges*, as well as editing *World Exchanges: Global Industry Outlook and Investment Analysis* and producing *Trading Places*.

World Exchanges is a quarterly publication offering the first comprehensive review with a global perspective on the financial performance and role of the leading listed international securities exchanges. *Trading Places* is a monthly publication carrying news and commentary about exchanges and trading venues worldwide.

Formerly a senior Reuters executive, Herbie has detailed technical knowledge of data management and information delivery systems, data standards, and the financial sector.

Mondo Visione Exchange Forum 2007 Speakers' Biographies

Paul Arlman was Secretary General of the Federation of European Securities Exchanges from 1998 to 2005. He is a founding Board Member of the European Corporate Governance Institute (ECGI). Between 2001 and 2003 he was Chairman of the Industry Advisory Committee to the European Parliamentary Financial Services Forum (EPFSF). From 1990 to 1997, he was the Secretary General of the Amsterdam Stock Exchange Association, and previously he was on the Board of the European Investment Bank in Luxembourg and worked for the Netherlands Ministry of Finance. In May 2005 Mr. Arlman was elected International Chair of Plan International, a globally active child-centered community development charity.

Robert Barnes joined the proprietary trading team at Swiss Bank Corporation in 1994, gaining experience on the LIFFE derivatives floor as a yellow jacket. He is currently Managing Director, Equities responsible for Market Structures at UBS Investment Bank. Dr. Barnes is Chairman of the Securities Trading Committee of the London Investment Banking Association and a member of the FSA's Capital Markets Sector Senior Practitioners Committee and of Euroclear's UK Market Advisory Committee. He is the UBS high level representative to the EU Commission's CESAME group.

Giovanni Beliossi is Managing Partner at FGS Capital LLP, where he is the CEO and responsible for portfolio management. Previously he was Associate Director of hedge funds at First Quadrant Ltd, where he established its pan-European long/short equity market neutral portfolios, and was responsible for UK-based hedge fund business. Previously he was a Research Fellow with the Economics Department of the University of Bologna, and he has held appointments with BARRA International and Eastern Group Plc. He is the European Chair of the Steering Group of the Investor Risk Committee (IRC) of IAFE working on guidelines for disclosure and transparency for hedge funds.

Peter Bennett was the architect and led the development of the information, trading and data exchange systems that underpinned the London Stock Exchange's move from floor to screen trading at the time of Big Bang. He went on to serve on the Managing Board of the Exchange for three years in the capacity of CIO. He then co-founded and was the architect of the Tradepoint Investment Exchange, now operating as virt-x. Following the sale of Tradepoint, Mr. Bennett has focussed on strategic consultancy work in capital markets. He is currently advising HCL Technologies, a major Indian systems integrator, about business development opportunities in Capital Markets.

Nigel Chapman is Director of the BBC World Service, responsible for the overall editorial leadership and management of the world's leading international radio broadcaster and its new media operations. He has worked for the BBC for more than 20 years. Mr. Chapman is also Chair of the Board of Trustees of Plan International (UK). Plan International is a globally active child-centered community development charity. Plan has 16 fundraising national organizations and invests in close to 50 developing countries, with a strong focus on the interests of children.

Luis Correia da Silva is Managing Director of Oxera Finance and has directed the company's work for the Financial Services Authority, London Stock Exchange, DTCC, Investment Management Association, Deutsche Asset Management, World Bank, European Asset Management Association, DTI, and various utilities and regulators. Dr. Correia da Silva has also directed policy and research studies for both the Competition Commission and OFT, and published extensively on economics and finance matters.

William F. Cruger is a Managing Director of JPMorgan responsible for investment banking business with Financial Institutions. In addition to these responsibilities, from 2000 to 2001 he oversaw the rationalization of the firm's private equity investments in trading platforms and related ventures and served on the boards of Archipelago, Credittrade and CapitalIQ. Previously, Mr. Cruger ran the firm's investment banking practices in Japan (1991–96), Latin America (1989–91), and Emerging Asia (1984–88).

Suzanne L. Dence is Managing Consultant responsible for research and thought leadership for the financial markets industry within IBM's business research group, the Institute for Business Value. She has presented IBM's research at numerous conferences throughout the world, including the Economist, China International Banking Convention, Seoul Financial Forum, as well to IBM's clients. Ms. Dence joined IBM in October 2000 from State Street Corporation, where she worked in the custody division of State Street Bank and in the investment management division of State Street Global Advisors. Previously she worked for Bank of America.

Donald F. Donahue is President and Chief Executive Officer for The Depository Trust & Clearing Corporation and for three of DTCC's operating subsidiaries. Prior to joining the depository in 1986, Mr. Donahue worked for five years for Barr Brothers & Co., Inc., a broker/dealer specializing in municipal securities. From May 2004 to June 2006, Mr. Donahue served as Chairman of the Financial Services Sector Coordinating Council for Critical Infrastructure Protection and Homeland Security, a private sector group that interacts with the Treasury Department and Federal and State regulators on infrastructure protection and homeland security issues.

Michelle Edkins is Managing Director at Governance for Owners (GO), an independent partnership between major financial institutions, shareowners and executives dedicated to adding value for long-term share owners by making use of ownership rights. She is responsible for GO's Stewardship Services and the governance and engagement policies that underlie them, working with clients and other institutional investors on a range of governance issues. Prior to joining GO, Ms. Edkins spent over 8 years at Hermes Pensions Management, initially as the head of the corporate governance team and latterly as Director of Institutional Relations.

Kevin Formby is Global Head of Provider and Segment Development at BT Radianz.

Joe Gawronski is the President and Chief Operating Officer of Rosenblatt Securities, an agency-only execution boutique founded in 1979. He was formerly a securities lawyer with Sullivan & Cromwell, a Vice President in the equities division with Salomon Smith Barney, and COO of Linx LLC, an alternative block trading system. He is an Allied Member of the NYSE, a member of the NYSE Hearing Board, a member of the Advisory Boards of both the *Journal of Trading* and *Wall Street & Technology* magazine, and a term member of the Council on Foreign Relations.

Martin Graham is the Director of Market Services at the London Stock Exchange and Head of AIM, the Exchange's market for smaller, growing companies. He is responsible for the market-facing functions within the Exchange, as well as the development of domestic and international markets services including client relationships, market operations, market regulation and RNS, the Exchange's regulatory news service. He has also assumed responsibility for the overall management of EDX (the London Stock Exchange's equity derivatives market). Prior to joining the LSE, Mr. Graham developed extensive industry experience as Managing Director and Global Head of Equity Sales at WestLB Panmure and Global Head of Equity Sales at Dresdner Kleinwort Benson.

David Hardy has been Head of Strategic Market Development since February 2007 at Man Financial, a provider of broking and clearing services and part of Man Group plc. He began his career with Barclays Bank Group and Barclays Merchant Bank. He was Chief Executive of LCH Clearnet and, prior to that, of London Clearing House (LCH) from 1987 until 2006. Mr. Hardy serves on the Board of the Institute for Financial Markets in the United States, and in the past has served on the Boards of the International Petroleum Exchange, the Futures and Options Association, the London Commodity Exchange, and the CFTC's Global Market Advisory Committee.

Christopher Hohn is Managing Director and Portfolio Manager of the London-based Children's Investment Fund, which he founded in 2004.

From 1996 to 2003 he was Portfolio Manager of Perry Capital, leading its European event-driven investment strategy. Previously he was an Associate at Apax Partners working with Jon Moulton (founder of Schroder Ventures) on special situation LBO's in Europe, and worked in the Corporate Finance Division of Coopers & Lybrand.

John Holland is Managing Director and Chief Operating Officer of UBS's Management Board for Global Cash Equities. He is also a Member of the UBS Investment Bank Board and chairs the Cash Operating Committee, with responsibility for prioritizing and executing the technology initiatives of the Cash Managing Board. Mr. Holland originally joined UBS in London in 1985 in the International Capital Markets Division as a member of the Asian origination team. He headed the Asian Equities Business from 2002, having previously relocated to Hong Kong to take up the role of Global Head of Asian Distribution.

Emma Hunt is a senior associate in Mercer's Investment Consulting business in London, where she supports clients on issues relating to responsible investment and shareholder engagement. Prior to joining Mercer Investment Consulting in June 2005, she spent two years heading up the Centre for Sustainable Investment at Forum for the Future, a UK-based think tank. Previously, Ms. Hunt spent four years as a senior analyst focused on governance and socially responsible investment with a UK-based global asset manager. She sits on a number of advisory committees, including the UK Social Investment Forum's Sustainable Pensions Advisory Board.

Phillip Hylander is Goldman Sachs' global head of Equities One-Delta Trading and co-head of the European equities franchise businesses, which include the One-Delta and derivatives businesses and client acquisition within Securities Services. He is also responsible for Equities Division investments in exchanges and financial infrastructure companies globally. Mr. Hylander joined Goldman Sachs in 2002 as co-head of Pan-European Shares. Previously, he worked for Deutsche Bank, where he ran its global (ex-US) Equity Trading business. He was also a member of its European Equities Executive Committee and was a board member of Morgan Grenfell & Co.

Sir Digby Jones served as Director-General of the Confederation of British Industry, the UK's 'Voice of Business,' from 1 January 2000 to 30 June 2006. During his appointment he took the British business message to 70 different countries, meeting on a regular basis political, business and media figures in the United Kingdom and around the world. In 1998 Sir Digby joined KPMG as vice chairman of Corporate Finance, acting as close adviser to many public companies across the United Kingdom and in KPMG's global markets.

Richard Kilsby is Executive Vice-President of AKJ Limited. He was previously Vice-Chairman of the virt-x stock exchange, CEO of Tradepoint, Director at Instinet, Executive Director at the London Stock Exchange, and Managing Director, COO of Global Investment Banking, Head of Finance Europe, and Head of Corporate Derivatives at Bankers Trust. He also worked as Vice-President at Charterhouse Bank and as a partner at Price Waterhouse. Mr. Kilsby is also chairman of 888 Holdings plc and a nonexecutive director of Collins Stewart plc and Tullet Prebon plc.

David Krell is a founder and President & CEO of International Securities Exchange. From 1997 to 1998 he was Chairman and co-founder of K-Squared Research, LLC, a financial services consulting firm. Previously Mr. Krell was Vice President, Options and Index Products, of the New York Stock Exchange, where he managed marketing, systems, and new product introductions for the division, and First Vice President at the Chicago Board Options Exchange, responsible for the management and operation of the Marketing and Sales Division. He is a Director on the Board of The Options Clearing Corporation.

Per E. Larsson became Chief Executive Officer of the Dubai International Financial Exchange (DIFX) in July 2006. From 1996 to 2003 he was President and Chief Executive of OMX, where he led successful mergers with the Stockholm Stock Exchange and Helsinki Exchanges, and previously President of OM Stockholm, the Group's derivatives arm. Since leaving OMX, Mr. Larsson has held a number of senior positions including Executive Chairman of Outsourced Supply Management AB and Executive Chairman of label specialist Nilorn AB.

Ruben Lee is the Founder and Chairman of the Oxford Finance Group, a research and consulting firm that concentrates on business, economic, legal, and regulatory aspects of commodity and financial markets. From 1989 to 1992, Dr. Lee was a Fellow of Nuffield College, Oxford University, where he specialized in financial economics and law. He worked from 1980 to 1984 in the capital markets in New York and London for Salomon Brothers International. Dr. Lee is on the Conseil Scientifique of the Autorité des Marchés Financiers in France, and previously sat on the Advisory Panel of Financial Services Experts, established by the Economics and Monetary Affairs Committee, European Parliament.

Olivier Lefebvre is a Member of the Management Committee of NYSE Euronext, where he is in charge of Regulation and European Affairs. After working as an academic and in the economic research department of the Generale Bank (now Fortis Bank), he became an advisor and then chief of staff to the Belgian Minister of Finance. In January 1996 he became Chairman of the Managing Board of the Brussels Stock Exchange, where he conducted the merger with the derivatives market (Belfox) and the central depository and settlement organization (CIK). In early 2000 Dr. Lefebvre was one of the founders of Euronext, becoming Executive Vice-President and Member of the Managing Board.

Roger Liddell is Group Chief Executive of LCH.Clearnet Group Limited with overall responsibility for the Group's strategic objectives and financial targets. He spent the first ten years of his career with British Coal before joining Citibank NA in 1989, where he held various roles from internal operations management consultant to head of Foreign Exchange Operations. In 1993 Mr. Liddell joined Goldman Sachs, becoming Managing Director in 1998 and Head of Global Operations in 2000. He has served on the Board of LCH.Clearnet Group Limited since 2005 and was a Director of Euroclear Plc from 2000 to 2005.

Russell Loubser is Chief Executive Officer of JSE Limited. Prior to his appointment at the JSE in 1997, he was Executive Director of financial markets at Rand Merchant Bank Limited (RMB), which he joined from Finansbank Limited in 1985. During 1987, he was part of the team that started the futures industry in South Africa. He was Chairman of SAFEX for 2 years and Deputy Chairman for 1 year. Mr. Loubser is a member of the King Committee on Corporate Governance and the Policy Board for Financial Services and Regulation. He serves on the Board of Directors of the World Federation of Exchanges and was Chairman of the World Federation of Exchanges' Working Committee from October 2002 to October 2004.

Walter L. Lukken has served as Commissioner of the Commodity Futures Trading Commission since 2002. He is chairman of the CFTC's Global Markets Advisory Committee, which advises the Commission on international policies affecting the futures industry, and he frequently represents the Commission before international organizations and forums, including the International Organization of Securities Commissions and the Committee of European Securities Regulators. Prior to joining the CFTC, Commissioner Lukken served as counsel on the professional staff of the US Senate Agriculture Committee, specializing in futures and derivatives markets.

Tony Mackay is President and Managing Director of Instinet Europe, where he has full operational and strategic responsibility for Instinet's European business. He joined Instinet in 1995 as Dealing Director for Asia Pacific based in Hong Kong and has held positions as President and CEO of Instinet Japan and Head of Instinet Asia, and Head of Equities for Instinet International. Mr. Mackay began his stockbroking career in 1980 in Australia and has worked for both traditional and electronic brokerage firms in Sydney, Hong Kong, London, and Tokyo.

Mark Makepeace is FTSE Group's Chief Executive and company founder. He established FTSE Group as an autonomous company in 1995, and has been responsible for the company's global expansion since. Under his leadership, FTSE Group has grown from a start-up company with nine employees to a world leader in the design and management of stock market indices. Mr. Makepeace began his career in the City in 1985 with London Stock Exchange, where he worked on the deregulation of London's equity markets—the "Big Bang."

Seth Merrin is founder and CEO of Liquidnet, a global trading system that enables money management institutions to trade large blocks of equities directly and anonymously. Liquidnet is the third technology firm that Mr. Merrin has started. Previously, he co-founded VIE Systems, Inc, a financial services application integration software company that was sold to New Era of Networks (NEON) in 1999. In 1985, he founded his first company, Merrin Financial, a developer of innovative institutional trading solutions which was sold to ADP in 1996. Prior to this, Mr. Merrin was a risk arbitrage trader for CIBC Oppenheimer.

Mario Nava is Head of the European Commission's Financial Markets Infrastructure Unit, which is responsible for regulation of the post-trading area in EU financial markets. His previous role was as a member of the Group of Policy Advisers to the EU Commission President, where he had particular responsibility for the EU budget and economic policy coordination between member states. Before joining the Group of Policy Advisers, Dr. Nava worked for the Commission's Taxation and Budget Departments and in the Cabinet of the Competition Commissioner, Prof. Mario Monti.

James E. Newsome has been President and CEO of the New York Mercantile Exchange since August 2004. Prior to that, he served as chairman of the Commodity Futures Trading Commission (CFTC) from December 2000, having been a commissioner of the CFTC since August 1998. In addition to his responsibilities at the CFTC, Dr. Newsome served as a member of the President's Working Group on Financial Markets and on the President's Corporate Fraud Task Force to coordinate corporate fraud investigations. He currently serves on the Board of Directors of the Dubai Mercantile Exchange, NYMEX Europe, and the National Futures Association.

Andreas Preuss is Chief Executive Officer of Eurex and a member of the Executive Board of Deutsche Börse AG, where he is responsible for Customers/Markets (Trading and Clearing Services). He is also Chairman of the Management Board of FWB Frankfurter Wertpapierbörse. Mr. Preuss returned to the Deutsche Börse Group in 2006 after four years as Chief Operating Officer, Member of the Board and Partner at Mako Group in London, and two years as President of Trading

Technologies International, Chicago. Previously he filled many senior management roles at DTB Deutsche Terminbörse, Deutsche Börse, and Eurex, after working for Dresdner Bank and Andersen Consulting.

Xavier R. Rolet is Managing Director, European Senior Client Relationship Management for Lehman Brothers International. Before joining Lehman Brothers in February 2000, he had worked for Goldman Sachs in New York and London, Credit Suisse First Boston and Dresdner Kleinwort Benson. He is Chairman of the Strategic Advisory Group of the London Stock Exchange, a member of Deutsche Börse's London Equity Market Advisory Committee and Euronext's London Advisory Group, a member of the Supervisory Board of MTS Group SpA, and a member of the European Securities Markets Expert Group (ESME) of the European Commission.

Mary L. Schapiro is Chairman and CEO of NASD, the primary regulator of 5,200 US securities brokerage firms and nearly 700,000 registered brokers. She joined NASD in 1996 as President of NASD Regulation and was named Vice Chairman in 2002. Previously, Ms. Schapiro was Chairman of the Commodity Futures Trading Commission and served for six years as a Commissioner of the Securities and Exchange Commission. She is an active member of the International Organization of Securities Commissions (IOSCO) and was Chairman of the IOSCO SRO Consultative Committee from 2002 until 2006.

Holly A. Stark is President and Managing Member of Efficient Frontiers LLC. Prior to this appointment she spent five years as Director of Trading and Principal at Kern Capital Management, a New York money management firm, following similar positions at Dalton, Greiner, Hartman, Maher & Co., and its predecessor firm, Dillon, Read Capital. During her career as a buy-side trader, Ms. Stark served on many advisory committees at NASDAQ and the New York Stock Exchange. She currently serves on the NASD's Market Regulation Committee, and the Board of the National Organization of Investment Professionals.

Peter Stockman is a partner in PA Consulting Group's Financial Services Practice, where he leads PA's capital markets group in New York. For the past 20 years he has worked in Europe and North America with investment banks, exchanges, clearing houses, energy companies and re-insurance companies on issues related to new product strategy, operational efficiency, and risk management. Mr. Stockman began his career at American Telephone and Telegraph, and prior to joining PA Consulting Group he was a partner with Accenture in that firm's Global Financial Markets and Global Resources (Energy) industry practices.

Brian Taylor is Chief Financial Officer and Head of IT at Plus Markets Group plc. He trained as an accountant, working for Arthur Andersen, Merrill Lynch and Price Waterhouse. His previous management roles have included Head of Finance for the Court Funds Office (Department for Constitutional Affairs) and Chief Executive Officer— Bahamas International Securities Exchange. In previous consulting roles Mr. Taylor has worked with SWX-virt-x, Liffe, UBS Warburg, OMX, Oslo Børs, Borsa Italiana, Euro MTS, FESE, SIA SpA, Bombay SE and the Ministry of Economy & Commerce, Qatar.

Robert H. Urtheil is a Principal in the Corporate and Institutional Banking Practice at management consultancy Oliver Wyman. Before joining Oliver Wyman, he was a director and Head of Market Development & Strategy with Deutsche Börse Group. In his previous role he was responsible for various corporate transactions and led projects in New York, Chicago, London, Luxembourg, and Frankfurt. Prior to that, Mr. Urtheil worked for an investment bank and an asset management firm.

Tony Weeresinghe is founder and Chief Executive Officer of Millennium Information Technologies Ltd, a Sri Lanka–based provider of innovative trading systems. His previous positions have included CEO of Open Systems Computerland, Country Manager for Oracle Data Management Systems Ltd, and Software Manager for Data Management Software Limited. Mr. Weeresinghe is also founder and Chairman of E-Channelling, the first e-commerce company in Sri Lanka.

Sir Nigel Wicks is the Chairman of both Euroclear plc and Euroclear SA/NV and a non-executive director of the Edinburgh Investment Trust plc. He served as non-executive Chairman of CRESTCo, the settlement system for UK and Irish securities, from 2001 until its merger with Euroclear in 2002. Sir Nigel was a member of the British Civil Service for 32 years. From 1989 to 2000, he was Second Permanent Secretary and Director of International Finance at HM Treasury. Before this, he spent periods as Principal Private Secretary to Prime Minister Margaret Thatcher, Economic Minister at the British Embassy in Washington DC, and as UK Executive Director at the World Bank and the IMF and as Private Secretary to Prime Ministers James Callaghan and Harold Wilson. He began his career at British Petroleum in 1958.

Patrick L. Young writes on capital market structures; his latest book *The Exchange Manifesto* has just been published. A passionate innovator, Mr. Young has been in the vanguard of introducing new products such as single stock futures and creating exchanges for the trading of contracts on sports and entertainment markets as well as various commodities, and he has consulted for many leading financial and governmental organizations. Currently Mr. Young is executive director of ODL Monaco SAM and Chairman of the Exchange Invest Conference Monaco, which takes place during September.

Index